Cambridge Elements 

Elements in American Politics
edited by
Frances E. Lee
Princeton University

SHIFTING ALLEGIANCES

The Election of Latino Republicans to Congress and State Legislatures

Robert D. Alvarez
Sam Houston State University

Jason P. Casellas
University of Houston

CAMBRIDGE
UNIVERSITY PRESS

Shaftesbury Road, Cambridge CB2 8EA, United Kingdom

One Liberty Plaza, 20th Floor, New York, NY 10006, USA

477 Williamstown Road, Port Melbourne, VIC 3207, Australia

314–321, 3rd Floor, Plot 3, Splendor Forum, Jasola District Centre,
New Delhi – 110025, India

103 Penang Road, #05–06/07, Visioncrest Commercial, Singapore 238467

Cambridge University Press is part of Cambridge University Press & Assessment,
a department of the University of Cambridge.

We share the University's mission to contribute to society through the pursuit of
education, learning and research at the highest international levels of excellence.

www.cambridge.org
Information on this title: www.cambridge.org/9781009533065
DOI: 10.1017/9781009533096

First published 2025

A catalogue record for this publication is available from the British Library

ISBN 978-1-009-53306-5 Hardback
ISBN 978-1-009-53308-9 Paperback
ISSN 2515-1606 (online)
ISSN 2515-1592 (print)

Shifting Allegiances

The Election of Latino Republicans to Congress and State Legislatures

Elements in American Politics

DOI: 10.1017/9781009533096
First published online: April 2025

Robert D. Alvarez
Sam Houston State University

Jason P. Casellas
University of Houston

Author for correspondence: Jason P. Casellas, jcasellas@uh.edu

Abstract: *Shifting Allegiances* provides a comprehensive analysis of the increasing presence and influence of Latino Republicans in Congress and state legislatures. Contrary to past assumptions, this Element reveals that Latino Republicans are a diverse group, no longer confined to Cuban Americans in South Florida. By examining election data and candidate characteristics since 2018, the authors uncover the factors contributing to the success of Latino Republicans, including district demographics, conservative values, and strategic campaigning. This shift in political dynamics highlights a broader trend of ideological realignment and offers insights into the evolving landscape of Latino political representation in the United States.

Keywords: Latino Republicans, Representation, Elections, Legislature, Majority-Minority Districts

ISBNs: 9781009533065 (HB), 9781009533089 (PB), 9781009533096 (OC)
ISSNs: 2515-1606 (online), 2515-1592 (print)

Contents

1 Introduction: Shifting Allegiances

In the aftermath of the 2020 election, pundits and journalists were perplexed at the number of Latinos who voted to reelect Donald Trump, especially in South Florida and South Texas. While the vast majority of Latinos still voted for President Joe Biden, the puzzle remains about the 27–30 percent of Latinos nationwide who have consistently supported Republicans in presidential elections (Corral and Leal, 2020; de la Garza and Cortina, 2007; Fraga et al., 2025; Saavedra Cisneros, 2016). Many thought that Trump's harsh rhetoric about Mexican immigrants, as well as his strict policies on immigration, would lead to a record-low in Latino votes for the Republican candidate and affect down-ballot candidates (Galbraith and Callister, 2020). This did not materialize, and in fact, since 2018, we have seen a growth of Latino Republicans running for and winning at both the state and federal levels in places one would not expect. This Element will explain why. Who are the Latino Republicans serving in Congress and state legislatures? How are they similar or different when compared to their Democratic Latino counterparts? This Element examines these questions and more.

Why are these questions important? Latinos currently constitute 19.5 percent of American society, and this percentage is likely to grow regardless of changes in American immigration policy. While research on public opinion and vote choices among Latinos who support Republicans is growing, we still know little about how these attitudes translate into Latino Republican candidacies, where they win, why they succeed, and how they govern once in office.

The second reason questions about Latino Republicans are important is that they reflect underlying questions about partisanship broadly conceived. Some might assume that the story of Latino Republicans parallels the story of Black Republicans. According to this view, Latino and Black Republicans are analogous in terms of their attitudes and beliefs. While there may be some similarities, there are also significant differences (Alvarez and García Bedolla, 2003; Chong and Kim, 2006; Sanchez and Masuoka, 2010). Latinos are a diverse and heterogeneous group, with immigration from various parts of Latin America (Abrajano and Alvarez, 2012; Bedolla, 2014; Bowler and Segura, 2012; Garcia, 2016). As this Element will uncover, Latino Republicans are also a diverse group and no longer constrained to the Cuban exile diaspora in Miami (Bishin and Klofstad, 2009; Dutwin et al., 2005).

This Element is the first systematic examination of the representation of Latino Republicans in Congress and State Legislatures in the United States. By examining a broad range of data sources, this Element answers an extensive array of timely and relevant political questions about the nation's largest ethnic group. We examine the election of Latino Republicans to Congress and State Legislatures since 2018. Only through examining a variety of legislators from different areas and contexts can we arrive at a rich account of Latino representation. The research methods employed here incorporate an eclectic use of materials to investigate the impact of several variables associated with representation, as well as other factors that have been largely overlooked in scholarly research on this topic.

1.1 Who Are Latino Republicans?

Scholars of Latino politics have long made the case that Latinos are not a monolithic group (Barreto and Segura, 2014; Bedolla, 2014; Garcia and Sanchez, 2015; Garcia, 2016). There is considerable diversity within the Latino community in terms of national origin, immigration experiences (if any), and political ideology and partisanship (Stewart, 2022). To be clear, most Latinos identify as Democrats and most Latino elected officials are Democrats (Barreto and Pedraza, 2009; Hajnal and Lee, 2011; Saavedra Cisneros, 2016). Indeed, since the 1960s, the majority of Latino Republican candidates for office have been Cuban American, mainly in South Florida (Girard et al., 2012). For Cuban exiles fleeing Castro's communist regime, the Republican Party and its conservative and anti-communist policies during the Nixon and later Reagan administrations appealed to the group and its immediate interest in opposing the Cuban regime (Bishin and Klofstad, 2011; Hill and Moreno, 1996). Although younger Cuban Americans are not as staunchly Republican, new waves of Latin Americans from Venezuela, in particular, have been courted by Republicans espousing anti-socialist views (Girard et al., 2012; Krogstad, 2014). Cadava (2020) traces the history of Latino Republicans and demonstrates the evolution of Republicanism in the various national-origin groups. Even in the largest Mexican American population, some states, such as New Mexico, have long elected Republicans to local and statewide offices. While the state as a whole has become more Democratic in recent years, some Republicans have been able to get elected at the state and local levels, most notably former governor Susana Martinez, a Republican.

We use the term "shifting allegiances" to show that, despite predictions that Latinos would abandon Republicans with the rise of Donald Trump in 2016 due to his rhetoric about immigration, there has actually been an increase in Latinos voting for Republicans since 2018, and correspondingly, Latino Republican candidates running for Congress and state legislative seats and winning said races.

In explanations of Latino support for Trump in 2016, scholars have found that his rhetoric on immigration actually appealed to a significant portion of the Latino community. Nearly three-fourths of Latino Trump voters were in favor of deporting all illegal immigrants. In addition, Latino voters were more conservative than the overall population of Latinos living in the United States, and other issues such as the economy, health care, and education were more important to Latino voters than immigration (Callister et al., 2019; Galbraith and Callister, 2020). In presidential races, 71 percent of Latinos supported Obama in 2012, 66 percent supported Hillary Clinton in 2016, and 59 percent supported Joe Biden in 2020 (McManus, 2022). Republicans have made efforts to translate this shift into state legislative and congressional seats, as Contreras (2022a) profiles with Republican Party recruitment of Latinos to run in districts that have historically had no interparty competition.

We do not observe a whole-scale abandonment of the Democratic Party as some Republican strategists might suggest, but at the same time, what is driving this increase is more Latino Republicans *running for legislative seats*, and, therefore, there is substantial growth in the number of Latino Republicans getting elected to office since 2018. Allegiances are indeed shifting, and Democrats would be better advised to ascertain why rather than deny or minimize this reality, as Jones-Correa et al. (2018) note in their review of recent trends in Latino politics.

This Element will show the empirical evidence of shifting allegiances among Latinos in terms of congressional and state legislative candidate emergence and subsequent elections. Other recently published work demonstrates that the shift to Republicans among Latinos between 2016 and 2020 did not constitute a fluke and appears to be sustained in 2022 (Fraga et al., 2025). Indeed, Trump improved on Mitt Romney's 2012 performance among key groups of Latinos (Protestants, low-income citizens, and the third generation). Moreover, Hillary Clinton underperformed Obama across multiple dimensions, and many Latino undecided voters and independents broke late for Trump in 2016 and appeared to stick with him in 2020 (Corral and Leal, 2020).

1.2 Latino Republican Representation

The first Latino to serve in the U.S. House of Representatives was a Republican. Romualdo Pacheco of California served that state in the late nineteenth century (Vigil, 1938). It was not until 1989 that the first Latina, Ileana Ros-Lehtinen of Florida, was elected to Congress. The representation of Latinos in Congress and subsequently in state legislatures only gradually grew until 1991, when redistricting efforts to create majority-minority districts led to an increase of Latinos serving in Congress (Lublin, 1997). Despite these efforts, the representation of Latinos in Congress and state legislatures has not been proportional to their population numbers (Casellas, 2011a; Rouse, 2013; Wilson, 2017).

In the post–World War II era, the first Latino Republican elected to Congress was Manuel Lujan of New Mexico, who served from 1969 to 1989. New Mexico was one of the few states that elected Latino Republicans to statewide and local offices in the mid-twentieth century, including, most recently, Governor Susana Martinez, who served from 2011 to 2019 (Casellas, 2011b). However, the only non-Cuban Latino Republican to serve in Congress between 1989 and 2011 was Henry Bonilla, who represented a rural Texas district between 1993 and 2007. In 2011, with the elections of Jaime Herrera Beutler of Washington, Raul Labrador of Idaho, and Bill Flores of Texas, non-Cuban Latino Republicans began to take office in the U.S. Congress to be followed by several more members in the ensuing years.

The study of political representation in legislatures began with a theoretical treatment by Pitkin (1967), further typologizing the concept into descriptive and substantive components. That is, descriptive representation occurs when legislators share the same demographic characteristics, while substantive representation involves shared political ideas and interests irrespective of demographics (Mansbridge, 1999). Empirical studies of representation have further expanded the role of each type of representation, with some scholars arguing that what truly matters is substantive representation (Swain, 1993), while others argue the importance of descriptive representation in yielding substantive representation (Bratton and Haynie, 1999; Dovi, 2002; Rouse, 2013).

Early work on Latino representation in Congress could not say much about Latino Republicans since none were in the chamber in the 1970s and 1980s when Combs et al. (1984) and Hero and Tolbert (1995) analyzed roll call votes. Casellas (2011b) examined to an extent the tradeoffs of descriptive representation and substantive representation and argues that scholars must look beyond simple demographics to examine how institutional contexts can shape the election of Latinos to legislatures and Congress. In particular, he finds some evidence that Latino Republicans were increasingly being recruited by the Republican Party to run in state legislative districts. In addition, Rouse (2013) shows variety in the emphasis legislators place on their ethnicity, especially by party affiliation.

The Congressional Hispanic Caucus was formed in 1976 and initially was composed of only Democrats. Early research on the CHC compared it to the Congressional Black Caucus, exploring similarities and differences (García, 2005; Jiménez, 2013; Johnson and Secret, 1996; Vigil, 1938-). While Ros-Lehtinen joined the caucus in 1990 upon her election to Congress, in 2007, when then Representative and caucus chair Xavier Becerra (D-CA) visited Cuba, the only Republicans in the caucus resigned en masse and formed their own alternative group called the Congressional Hispanic Conference (Morini, 2013). In 2017, moderate Cuban American Carlos Curbelo (R-FL) applied for membership to the Congressional Hispanic Caucus, but his membership was rejected due to his policy views (Caygle, 2017).

This Element explores the growth of Latino Republicans running and winning in state legislative districts and Congress. Early work on representation did not examine data on who was running in addition to who was winning in such districts, but here we examine both stages in the process (Lublin, 1997). Moreover, since the 2000s, a significantly more extensive and diverse pool of candidates and winners has emerged in state legislative races, warranting new analyses examining both descriptive and substantive representation (Dyogi-Phillips, 2021; Reingold et al., 2020).

1.3 Why the Growth in Latino Republicans Running?

As Latinos move to all parts of the country, we have observed the growth of candidates running for office in states with historically low Latino populations. In many of these instances, the candidates are Republicans who often do not advertise or make note of their Latino heritage. Indeed, it is still the case that only 13 percent of all Latino state lawmakers are Republican (Contreras, 2022a). Between 2018 and 2020, despite an increase in 87 Latino Republican candidates, the percentage of those candidates elected only grew by 2 percent, from 24 percent in 2018 to 26 percent in 2020. This proportion will undoubtedly increase as more Latino Republicans run for office. In fact, some work suggests that there is no evidence that Latinos running as Republicans do more poorly than White Republicans (Shah et al., 2022; White et al., 2022). The challenge in the past has been the supply of candidates running for office. As Gonzalez Juenke (2014) showed with data from the 2000s, once candidate self-selection is taken into account, the probability of electing a Latino to state legislatures increases substantially.

While in the past, the vast majority of Latino Republican candidates and victors were of Cuban American background, since 2018, we have seen a growth of non-Cuban Republican candidates emerge. In particular, Puerto Ricans outside of New York, historically the most Democratic of Latino voters, have emerged as Republican candidates for legislative seats (Madrid, 2018). This is especially the case in the Orlando area, which has the second largest population of Puerto Ricans outside of Puerto Rico. Starting with John Quinones, a Puerto Rican Republican legislator in the 2000s (Casellas, 2011b), more have begun to run for the legislature and win in central Florida seats (Salomon and Torrens, 2018). To be precise, more Latino Republicans are getting elected to office because more are running in all kinds of districts, from majority-minority districts to majority White districts.

1.3.1 What Makes Latino Republican Candidates Successful?

We identify several key factors contributing to the surge in Latino Republican candidates and subsequent success, including changing district characteristics, conservative values, religion, and GOP efforts to recruit Latino Republicans. Moreover, Latino Republicans are winning in majority White districts with low Latino populations, and we find that many Latino Republican legislators strategically decide to conceal their ethnicity. We demonstrate that the reach and diversity of Latino Republican candidates are much greater than previously anticipated and reflect a significant group that might influence future elections in many localities and challenge conceptions of Latino representation. We draw on data concerning district demographics, congressional and state legislative ideology, and candidate characteristics to establish who Latino Republican candidates are, who runs, who wins, the kinds of districts they represent, and the issues they prioritize across the United States.

1.4 Outline of This Element

Section 2 addresses the transformation of Latino Republican representation by examining Latino Republican candidates for state legislatures and Congress and providing insight into who they are. Extant literature suggests that Latino Republican candidates are traditionally of Cuban background, disproportionately male, and primarily limited to Florida, New Mexico, and Texas (Casellas, 2011b). Using the 2018 and 2020 Cooperative C3 data sets, this section uses descriptive data to illustrate how Latino Republican candidates have changed over recent election cycles, paying close attention to the geographic distribution of such candidates, their sub-ethnic composition, the number of Latina candidates, and the types of candidates who see the most success. In doing so, we uncover several possible causal mechanisms informing the increasing reach and diversity of Latino Republican candidates for state legislatures and outline our theory of Latino Republican candidate emergence and electoral success. We then use predictive models to explore the factors determining which Latino Republicans are successful and whether regional differences exist in who runs and who wins.

Section 3 adds measures for legislator ideology and candidate ideology (at the federal level) to judge the efficacy of ideology as a predictor for Latino Republican electoral success. An added benefit of using legislator ideology is that it allows us to see how Latino Republicans differ ideologically from Republicans of other ethnicities. Our findings show that Latino Republican legislators are, on average, the most conservative group among Republican legislators, with Latinas exhibiting particularly high levels of conservatism when compared to other groups. Furthermore, we find that Latino Republican legislators show higher levels of ideological extremity in districts that feature lower proportions of Latino residents. We conclude the section by discussing how ideology might make Latino Republican candidates more attractive and relatable to Republican voters in districts with low Latino populations.

Section 4 identifies emerging trends among Latino Republican candidates from our analyses and addresses several notable outliers. First, we discuss what the increasing diversity and reach of Latino Republican candidates mean for the future of the GOP and American politics. Equally important is how ideological movement among Latino Republican candidates and across districts changes our understanding of Latino representation. Latino majority districts moving toward the right implies that the Latino electorate is likely to become more of an electoral wildcard going forward. We then explore the increased success of Latino Republicans in districts with low Latino populations in greater detail. Through examining the campaign materials of Latino Republican candidates in districts with few Latinos, we identify several cases in which candidates conceal or ignore their heritage and instead stress religion and conservative values. This poses a challenge for how we conceptualize representation, as it raises the question: if a Republican candidate is found to be Latino despite attempting to remove their ethnicity from their campaign altogether, would it be disingenuous to describe that candidate as representative of Latinos? Moreover, it makes classifying the ethnicity of Latino Republican candidates extremely difficult, which in turn could prevent researchers from acquiring an accurate depiction of Latino representation, especially at the state level.

In sum, we demonstrate how the reach and diversity of Latino Republican candidates have grown considerably and reflect a significant group that might influence future elections and change our understanding of Latino representation. We situate the findings and contributions of this Element in the context of the broader literature on Latino representation.

2 Latino Republican Candidates: Who Are They?

The growth of the Latino electorate and shifting votes toward Republican candidates in elections has caught the attention of policymakers and political analysts. Most of the analysis of this phenomenon is trying to explain why some Latinos vote for Republican candidates for office, and the assumption is often that they are voting for White Republican candidates. While this is the case in most instances, this section explores the emergence and determinants of success of Latino Republican candidates for state legislative seats and the U.S. Congress. No longer can we assume that the only successful Latino Republican legislators are Cuban American men from South Florida. The landscape has changed, and this section will show that, since 2018, Latino Republican candidates are running and winning in all areas of the country and much of this growth is driven by non-Cuban Latinas.

In 2020, former schoolteacher Rosilicie Ochoa Bogh became the first Republican Latina elected to the California State Senate and the first person of Latino descent to win California's 23rd State Senate district. In addition to receiving the highest vote total of any candidate in the district's history, her victory was accompanied by a 31 percent increase in voter turnout from 2016 to 2020 (California State Senate District 23, 2021). Senator Ochoa Bogh's case is indicative of a national trend in which Latino Republicans are running for office both in greater numbers and in places where they normally are not on the ballot. With this example in mind, we examine recent data showing the growth of Latino Republican candidates in state legislatures in the United States. We focus on Latino Republican candidates for several reasons. First, we know very little about what explains who, why, and where Latino Republicans run for office and what those who are successful have in common. What we know is based on outdated anecdotal observations that most of the Latino Republicans running for office were Cuban American and isolated to Florida. While this perception is historically accurate to a certain extent, this does not explain more recent and noteworthy developments. By examining these candidates and winners, we can give rise to testable hypotheses about the determinants of the election of Latino Republicans to state legislatures and discover key differences that might be missed in large-scale examinations devoid of an in-depth understanding of this emerging group. In addition, given media attention about more Latinos voting for Republican candidates for many offices, such analyses are essential to understand the types of candidates running for office, what appeals they make to voters, and how they tailor their messages.

2.1 Latino Republicans

In terms of representation, Latinos are still descriptively underrepresented compared to their population (Casellas, 2011b). In the U.S. Senate, there are only six Latinos, one of whom is Cuban American and two are Republicans. This is not representative of the overall Latino population in terms of partisanship and national origin. That said, the six latino U.S. senators are prime examples of politicians who were able to appeal to non-Latino constituencies. The U.S. House is somewhat more representative, with the Congressional Hispanic Caucus (CHC) and the Congressional Hispanic Conference containing thirty-eight Democrats and eleven Republicans, respectively, mainly from California, Texas, and the Southwest.

At the state level, more than sixty-five Latinos represented districts without Latino majorities in 2009 and Latino Republicans have begun to win in districts without Latino majorities (Casellas, 2011b). This number has grown as more Latinos win in districts without Latino majorities. This includes Latinos who are not obviously Latino (have Anglo names), represent strongly Democratic or Republican districts, or were first appointed to their seats (Casellas, 2011b). In many cases, even many Latino representatives who come from majority White districts still embrace a Latino identity. Mario Goico, a Cuban American Republican from Kansas, for instance, reported how he helped block a bill that would have required undocumented students to pay out-of-state tuition in Kansas universities (Casellas, 2011b).

While the Democratic Party continues to feature more Latino lawmakers at both the national and state levels, strong Republican efforts to recruit and develop Latino candidates look to upset this balance in the near future. Furthermore, House Republicans have recently targeted Democratic-held districts with sizable Latino populations, with the National Republican Congressional Committee noting that twenty-nine of its seventy-five House-targeted districts in the 2022 midterms had a Latino population of over 15 percent (Kraushaar, 2022). These efforts were beginning to see results, as evidenced by Mayra Flores' June 2022 special election victory in which she became the first Mexican-born congresswoman and the first Republican to win Texas' 34th district. She subsequently lost against moderate Democrat Vicente Gonzalez in November 2022 but rechallenged him in the 2024 elections.

The influence of the Republican Party's Latino push is also present at the state level, with several states featuring a record number of Latino Republican candidates in 2022 (Contreras, 2022a, 2022b). Our results reflect many of these recent trends, showing that the growing number of Latino Republican candidates in state legislative elections are well distributed across the United States, increasingly Latina, and represent various national-origin groups. Given previous literature on the success of Cuban Americans in politics, we still believe that Cuban Republicans will be more likely to win legislative seats even though more non-Cubans are running. This is because of longer political incorporation in the Republican Party (Bishin and Klofstad, 2011; Moreno, 2006). We also argue that Latino Republicans outside of Florida and, to a certain extent, Texas will be more likely to run and win in majority White districts. This is because Republicans have been increasingly willing to vote for non-White candidates who espouse conservative viewpoints (Grossmann and Hopkins, 2024). Finally, in line with previous research showing that Latinas are more likely to appeal to White voters than Latinos, we expect Latina Republicans to perform better in majority White districts (Bejarano, 2013, 2014). We test the following hypotheses concerning the election of Latino Republicans to state legislatures and Congress based on the discussion earlier:

> **Cuban Republican Advantage** *Hypothesis 1: Despite the growth of non-Cuban Latino Republicans running, Cuban Republicans are more likely to win legislative seats.*
>
> **Majority White District Advantage** *Hypothesis 2: Latino Republicans are more likely to run and win in majority White districts.*
>
> **Latina Republican Advantage** *Hypothesis 3: Latina Republicans are more likely to win when they run than Latino Republican men.*

2.2 Data on Congressional and State Legislative Candidates, 2018–2020

We examine the racial/ethnic and gender composition of state legislative and congressional candidates and eventual congressional and state legislative winners from 2018 to 2020, focusing on Latino Republican candidates. To analyze elections involving Latino Republican candidates, we use congressional and state legislative candidate data from most states with legislative elections in 2018 and 2020, with the datasets covering forty-five and forty states, respectively, for the state legislatures and all states for Congress. We also use aggregate data from NALEO in a few of our descriptive analyses to further illustrate Latino candidate growth over the years.

The data on state legislatures is derived from the Candidate Characteristics Collaborative (C3) dataset (Fraga et al., 2020; Shah et al., 2022; White et al., 2022). The dataset was cooperatively coded, using information concerned with the name and district of each individual to determine race/ethnicity and gender by examining available relevant data about state legislative candidates in 2018 and 2020 (Fraga et al., 2020). Our congressional candidate dataset was made to mirror our state legislative data as closely as possible. To that end, we obtained a list of all Congress candidates from the FEC and added values for race/ethnicity, gender, election outcomes, and other control variables also featured in our state legislative data.

We further coded each Latino legislator's specific national origin group (Cuban, Mexican, Puerto Rican, Dominican, etc.) where the information was available. This process involved checking the social media sites of every candidate in the dataset to determine if any Latino candidates were missed in the initial coding process, if any Latino Republican candidate indicated their specific national origin group, and the election outcomes for all Latino Republican candidates. Religious affiliation was also coded where available; however, the findings were excluded from this analysis due to the difficulty of ascertaining this information.

Our comparative analysis looks at the differences in Latino Republican candidates from 2018 to 2020, examining geographic distribution and gender differences while also analyzing the ethnic distribution of Latino Republican candidates and how the election outcomes for Latinos vary from state to state. The C3 dataset began in 2018, which is why we do not include data from previous years aside from the aggregate data we found from 2016. Data on candidates before 2018 is not readily available. Lastly, we add state and congressional district demographics data from the U.S. Census Bureau to conduct preliminary regression analyses. We show our results through a series of tables, graphs, and maps using both count and proportion data.

2.3 Growth of Latino Republicans Running for Office Since 2018

Table 1 shows the distribution of Latino congressional candidates across party lines in the 2018 and 2020 elections. The 2020 elections featured a total of sixty-five Latino candidates, a six-candidate increase from the fifty-nine candidates who ran in the 2018 elections. The 2020 elections saw a significant increase in the number of Latino Republican candidates running for Congress, gaining ten candidates from 2018, whereas four fewer Latino Democrats ran for Congress in 2020 than in 2018.

We see similar results at the state level; Table 2 shows the distribution of Latino state legislative candidates across party lines in the 2018 and 2020 state legislative elections. The 2020 elections featured a total of 671 Latino candidates, a 113-candidate increase from the 558 Latino candidates who ran in the 2018 elections. While both parties had more Latino candidates running in 2020, the Republican Party experienced a much more pronounced increase in 2020, gaining 87 additional candidates compared to the Democrats' 26.

These results illustrate the growing power of Latinos within American politics; the overall increase at the state level indicates that the surging Latino population

Table 1 Party breakdown of Latino candidates for Congress (2018 and 2020)

Party	Count (2016)	Percentage of Latino Candidates (2016)	Count (2018)	Percentage of Latino Candidates (2018)	Count (2020)	Percentage of Latino Candidates (2020)
Latino Democrats	39	67.24%	41	69.5%	37	56.9%
Latino Republicans	19	32.2%	18	30.5%	28	43.1%
Grand Total	58		59		65	

Table 2 Party breakdown of Latino candidates for state legislature (2018 and 2020)

Party	Count (2016)	Percentage of Latino Candidates (2016)	Count (2018)	Percentage of Latino Candidates (2018)	Count (2020)	Percentage of Latino Candidates (2020)
Latino Democrats	295	76%	423	75.8%	449	66.9%
Latino Republicans	95	24%	135	24.2%	222	33.1%
Grand Total	390		558		671	

across the United States is beginning to translate into a growing number of Latino candidates for state legislatures, whereas the Republican Party's double-digit percentage increases in the share of Latino candidates at both the state and congressional levels possibly suggests the beginnings of a partisan shift among Latinos who choose to run for office. The gains of Latino candidates within the Republican Party are further explored in Tables 3 and 4, which look at changes in Republican candidate share across racial categories.

At the state level, Latinos are second only to White Republican candidates, albeit a large difference in numbers. Latinos saw the most significant increase in both total candidates and share, accounting for 4.82 percent of all Republican candidates in 2020 compared to 2.16 percent in 2018 at the state legislative level.

Table 3 Republican candidates for state legislature (2018 and 2020)

Race	Count (2018)	Percentage of Republican Candidates (2018)	Count (2020)	Percentage of Republican Candidates (2020)
Asian	65	1.04%	67	1.45%
Black	143	2.29%	86	1.87%
Latino	135	2.16%	222	4.82%
Native American	8	0.13%	11	0.24%
White	5,904	94.39%	4,222	91.62%
Grand Total	6,255		4,608	

Table 4 Republican candidates for Congress (2018 and 2020)

Race	Count (2018)	Percentage of Republican Candidates (2018)	Count (2020)	Percentage of Republican Candidates (2020)
Asian	10	2.38%	5	1.24%
Black	19	4.51%	30	7.44%
Latino	18	4.28%	28	6.95%
Native American	2	0.48%	2	0.50%
White	372	88.36%	338	83.87%
Grand Total	421		403	

We see similar results at the congressional level, with Latino candidates increasing by over 3 percent in 2020, accounting for nearly 7 percent of the Republican candidate share, compared to the roughly 4 percent candidate share seen in 2018. While the growth experienced by Latino Republican candidates in 2020 is significant, it is essential to determine where that growth is distributed and the factors informing it.

2.3.1 Latino Republican Candidates Well Distributed across the United States

In previous election cycles, Latino Republican candidates tended to be concentrated in Florida, New Mexico, and Texas. As Figures 1 and 2 illustrate, while the aforementioned states maintained high numbers of Latino candidates in 2020, the remaining Latino candidates are well distributed across the United States in states with both high and low Hispanic populations. This is also true at the congressional level, with Latino Republican candidates of numerous national origins running in many states, but mainly in California, Florida, and Texas.

While Latino Republican candidates enjoyed increased distribution across the board, Arizona, California, Colorado, Florida, New Mexico, New York, and Texas all saw significant increases in Latino Republican candidates at the state level. These results are somewhat unsurprising given the moderate to large Latino population in those states; however, the findings in some states featuring low Latino populations were significant, such as in the Midwest and Mountain West. Minnesota, Wisconsin, and Wyoming featured nine, six, and four Latino Republican candidates for state legislature, respectively, despite Latinos accounting for less than 10 percent of each state's population. Montana, which has a Latino population accounting for 3 percent of the state's total population, had six Latino Republican candidates running for office in 2020, with three winning. As Figure 3 illustrates, there are many other states with low Latino populations that featured a Latino Republican candidate in 2020. We believe that this speaks to a growing ideological congruency between portions of the Latino electorate.

Although the increased number of Latino Republican candidates and their wide-ranged distribution in 2020 each represent significant developments, whether these changes translate into election wins is an entirely different matter. As Table 5 shows, fifty-nine Latino Republican candidates, or roughly 26.5 percent of those who ran, were able to win state legislative seats. At the congressional level, a slightly higher 28.6 percent of Latino Republican candidates won.

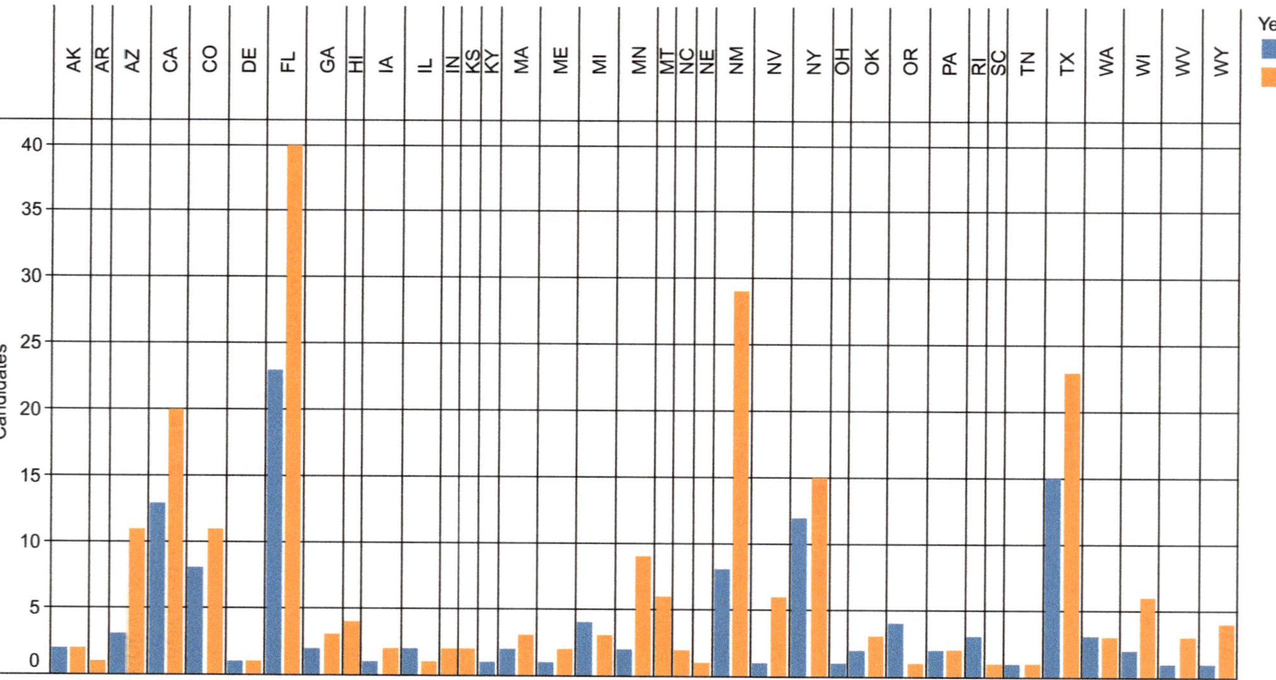

Figure 1 Latino Republican candidates: State legislatures (2018 and 2020)

Table 5 Latino Republican general election outcomes

	Congress				State		
Election Outcome	Female	Male	Grand Total	**Election Outcome**	Female	Male	Grand Total
Lost	28.57%	42.86%	71.43%	**Lost**	28.38%	45.05%	73.42%
Won	11.43%	17.14%	28.57%	**Won**	8.56%	18.02%	26.58%

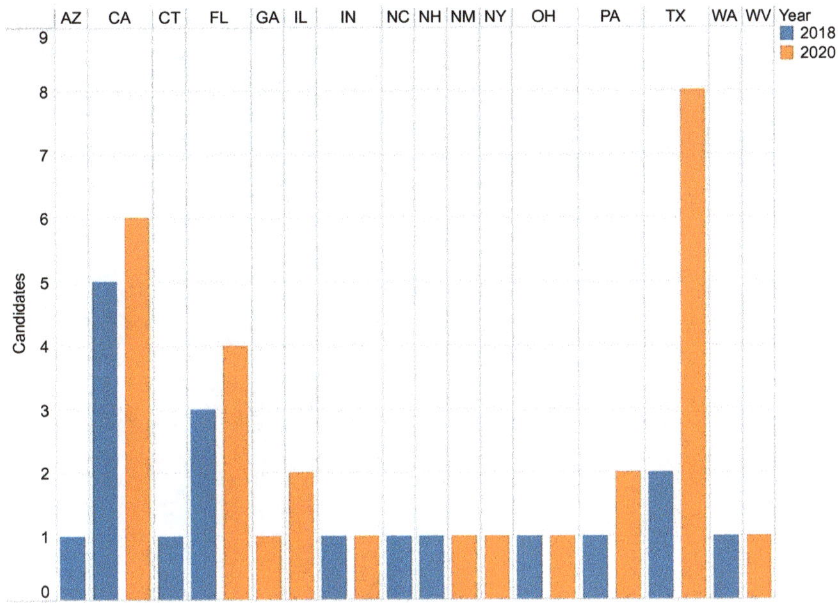

Figure 2 Latino Republican candidates: Congress (2018 and 2020)

This is a relatively modest increase over the 24 percent (32) of Latino Republican candidates who won in 2018. That said, a 27-candidate increase still signals what looks to be the start of a possible trend, and it is again important to consider the distribution of Latino Republican candidates. Figures 4 and 5 illustrate the state-by-state distribution of election outcomes involving Latino Republican candidates at the state legislative and congressional levels.

At the state level, the distribution of Latino Republican election winners is much more balanced than conventional wisdom would suggest. Consider Texas: despite featuring twenty-three candidates, only one of those candidates

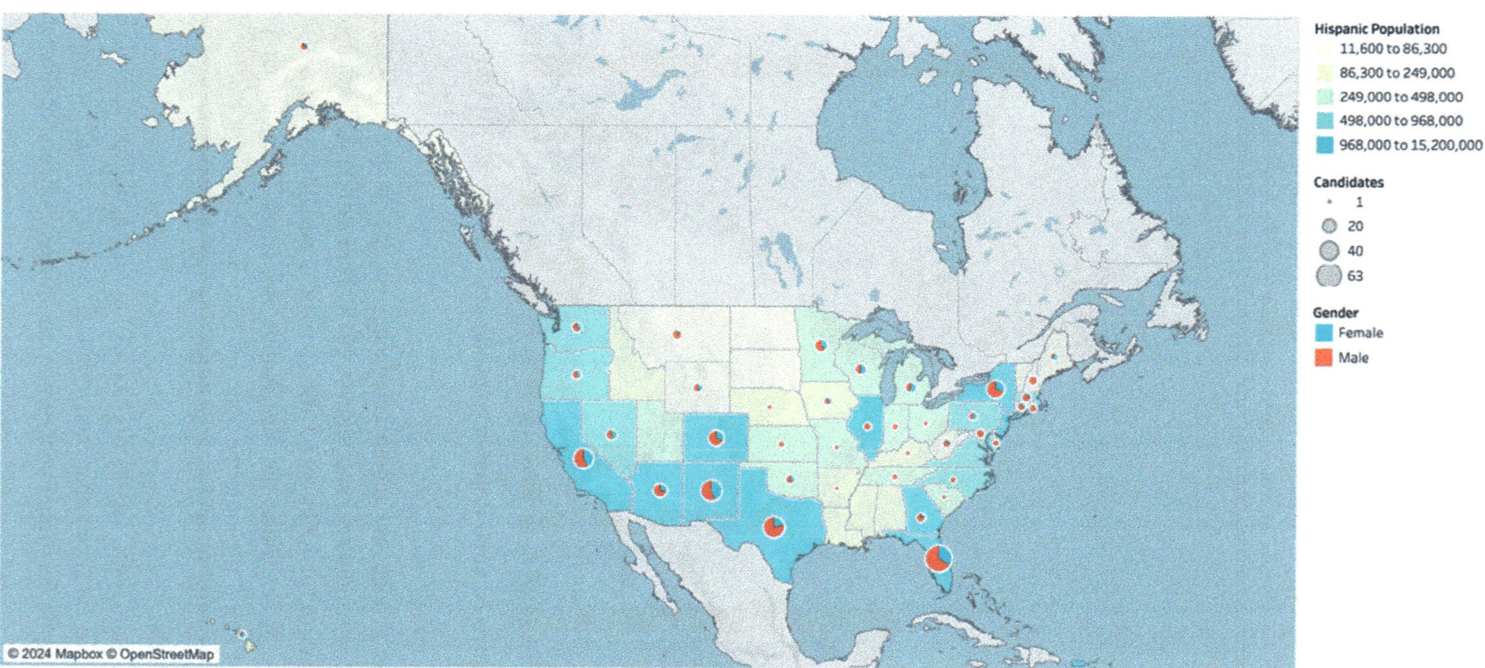

Figure 3 Distribution of Latino Republican candidates in 2020: State legislature

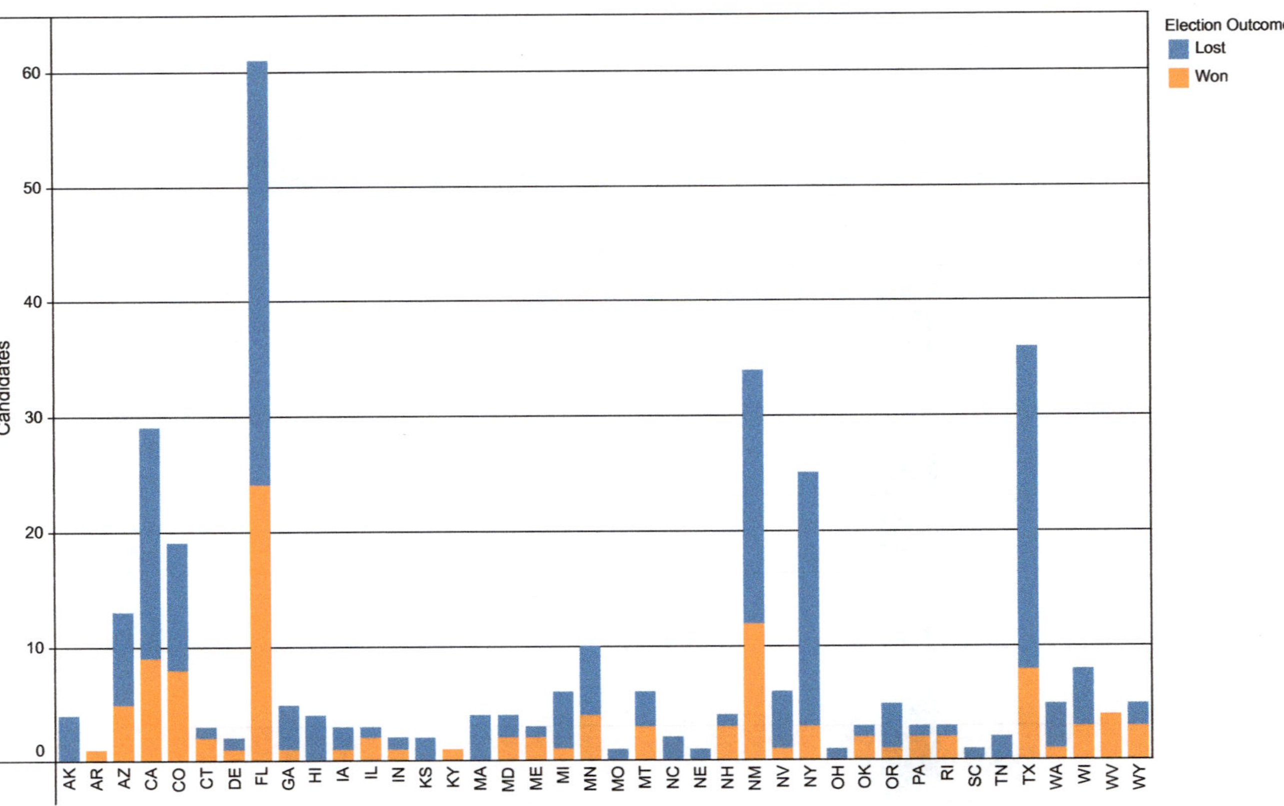

Figure 4 2020 election outcomes for Latino Republicans: State legislature

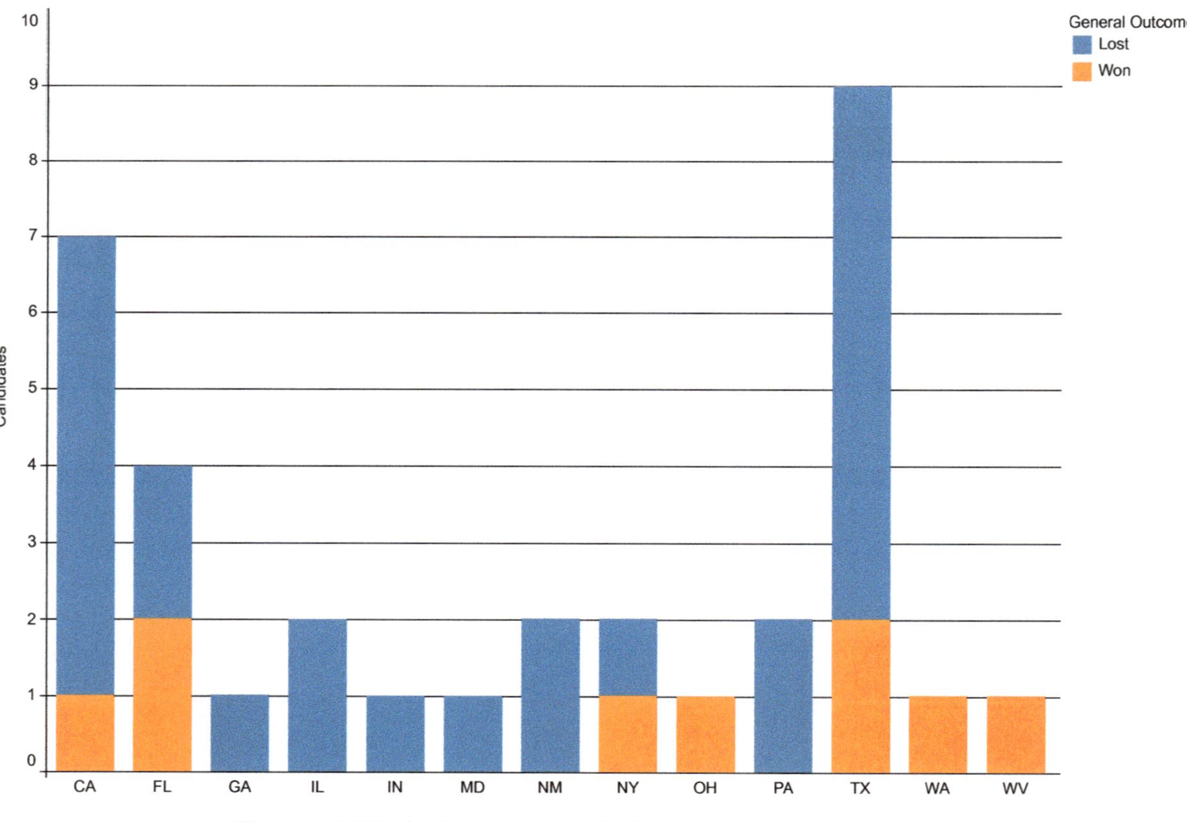

Figure 5 2020 election outcomes for Latino Republicans: Congress

won in their general election at the state legislative level. It was a similar story in Congress, where only two of the nine candidates succeeded.

The same goes for New Mexico, despite a plethora of Latino Republican candidates to choose from, very few won seats in the state legislature. At the congressional level, the two Latina candidates running in separate districts lost to Democrats. On the other hand, multiple states not often associated with Latino populations produced several Latino Republican legislators in 2020, with candidates from Wyoming, West Virginia, Wisconsin, Montana, and Minnesota, among others, all featuring more Latino legislators than Texas. This may be due to greater acceptance of Latino Republican candidates in states outside the South and Southwest. Regardless, it shows that Republican Latino candidates now have a better chance of winning elections in many states where they seldom ran previously. In much the same way the literature on women in politics demonstrates that when women run, they win, we observe that when Latino candidates run, they often do well in regions in which we do not expect such candidates (Bejarano, 2013, 2014; Lawless and Fox, 2008, 2010, 2018).

2.3.2 Latino Republicans More Likely to Lose as Share of Latinos in District Increases

Our regression analyses, illustrated in Tables 6 and 7, support the idea that Latinos are experiencing greater success in areas where they are not expected to. Latino Republican candidates are more likely to win in districts with lower Latino populations compared to districts with higher populations.

Even after controlling for incumbency and legislative chambers, higher proportion Latino populations maintain their negative relationship with electoral success among Latino Republicans at the state level. Furthermore, as Model 2 of Table 7 shows, this relationship is also present when accounting for primary elections at the congressional level.

As depicted in Figure 6, Latino Republican candidates are more likely to lose in districts with higher proportions of Latino residents. We observe a stark partisan difference in the determinants of electoral success among Latino candidates for state legislature and Congress. Democrats benefit significantly from a higher proportion of Latinos in districts, whereas Republicans do not. The fact that Latino Republican candidates are more likely to get elected in districts with lower Latino populations suggests that the way Latinos are viewed among Republicans is shifting. Alternatively, other candidate characteristics are perceived as more important than candidate ethnicity.

Table 6 Determinants of electoral success: State legislature

	Electoral Success	
	(1)	**(2)**
Latino Population	0.478^{***}	0.122^{*}
	(0.088)	(0.069)
GOP	0.086	0.050
	(0.071)	(0.054)
Upper chamber		0.069^{**}
		(0.033)
Incumbent		0.695^{***}
		(0.032)
Latino Population*GOP Candidate	-0.679^{***}	-0.235^{**}
	(0.149)	(0.115)
Constant	0.251^{***}	0.135^{***}
	(0.047)	(0.037)
N	675	675
R^2	0.085	0.467
Adjusted R^2	0.081	0.463
Residual Std. Error	0.471 (df = 671)	0.360 (df = 669)
F Statistic	20.837^{***} (df = 3; 671)	117.039^{***} (df = 5; 669)

$^{*}p < .1$; $^{**}p < .05$; $^{***}p < .01$

2.3.3 Cuban American Republicans Still More Likely to Win Seats than non-Cuban Latinos

Another critical dimension to consider when addressing the growth of Latino Republican candidates is the many different national origin groups that fall under the umbrella of the catch-all term "Latino." Latino Republican candidates have historically been of Cuban background or Mexican Americans from the American Southwest. Our findings, shown in Figures 7 and 8, feature the expected high numbers of Cuban Americans and Mexican Americans and also illustrate ethnic variation across several groups, with Puerto Ricans representing an extensive group among Latino Republicans, a novel finding given the traditional attachment of Puerto Ricans to the Democratic Party (LNS, Latino National Political Survey).

While Argentineans, Colombians, and Salvadorans were robustly represented in relation to their percentages of the U.S. Latino population, Puerto Ricans and Mexicans stand out in particular. Although the latter group is the country's largest national origin Latino group, their state distribution in 2020 was quite surprising.

Table 7 Determinants of electoral success: Congress

	General Election	Primary Election
	(1)	(2)
Latino Population	0.583[***]	0.677[***]
	(0.185)	(0.233)
GOP	0.131	0.268[*]
	(0.115)	(0.145)
Latino Population*GOP	−0.679[***]	−0.645[**]
	(0.240)	(0.303)
Constant	0.021	0.104
	(0.093)	(0.117)
N	182	182
R^2	0.096	0.046
Adjusted R^2	0.081	0.030
Residual Std. Error (df = 178)	0.383	0.483
F Statistic (df = 3; 178)	6.336[***]	2.867[**]

$*p < .1; **p < .05; ***p < .01$

While the majority of Republican candidates with Mexican ancestry ran in New Mexico, Texas, and California, they were represented in over twenty states, going against historical expectations that Mexican Republicans are limited to a few states. Puerto Ricans are historically considered a Democratic group, and yet they account for nearly 20 percent of Latino Republican candidates at the state legislative level, yet a smaller proportion at the congressional level. Furthermore, they are featured in more states than Cuban candidates, with candidates in seventeen states and over five candidates in both Florida (six) and New York (eight). These findings speak to changes in Latino candidate emergence, and while the causes of this change are undetermined, we suspect religious affinity with the Republican Party may be a contributing factor, as evangelicals have made significant inroads among Puerto Rican communities in recent years (Pew Research Center, 2018; Winter, 2021). The number of Puerto Rican Republicans running at the congressional level in 2020 was fairly small (seven), but this will undoubtedly increase in years to come.

Cuban Americans, as expected, account for over 25 percent of Latino Republican candidates at the state level and over 30 percent at the congressional level despite only accounting for 4 percent of the Latino population in the United States. Unlike in previous years, however, Cubans ran in twelve different states,

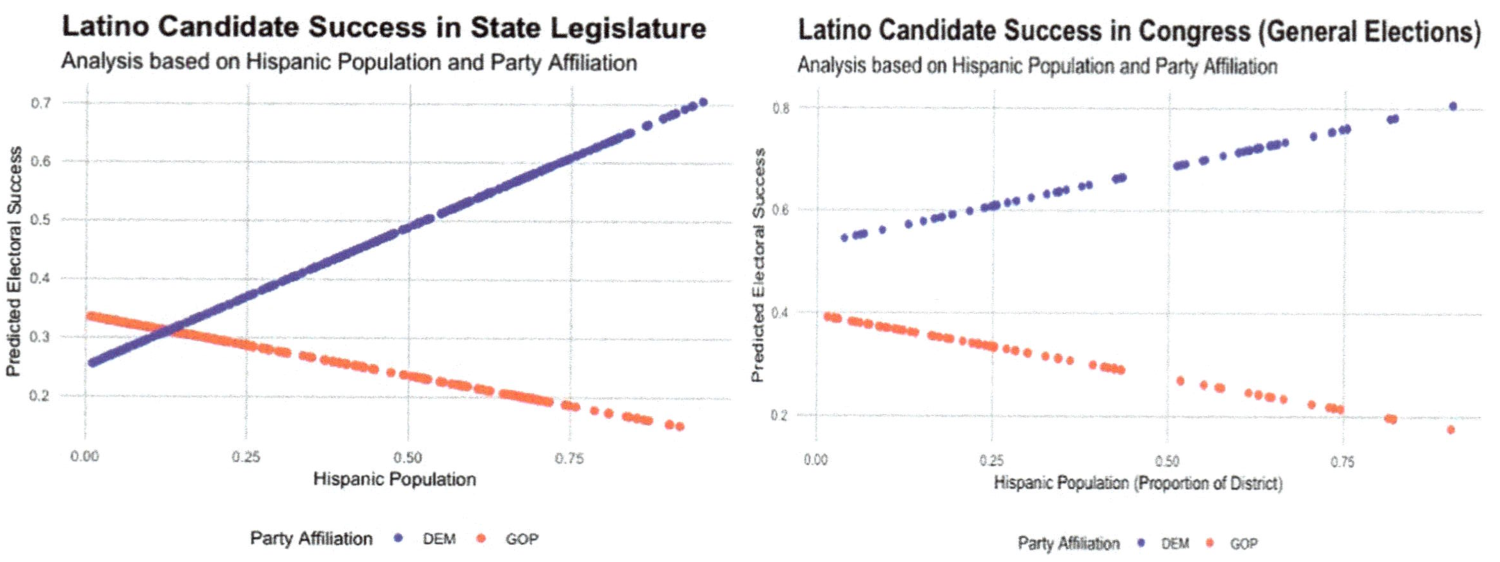

Figure 6 Latino candidate success

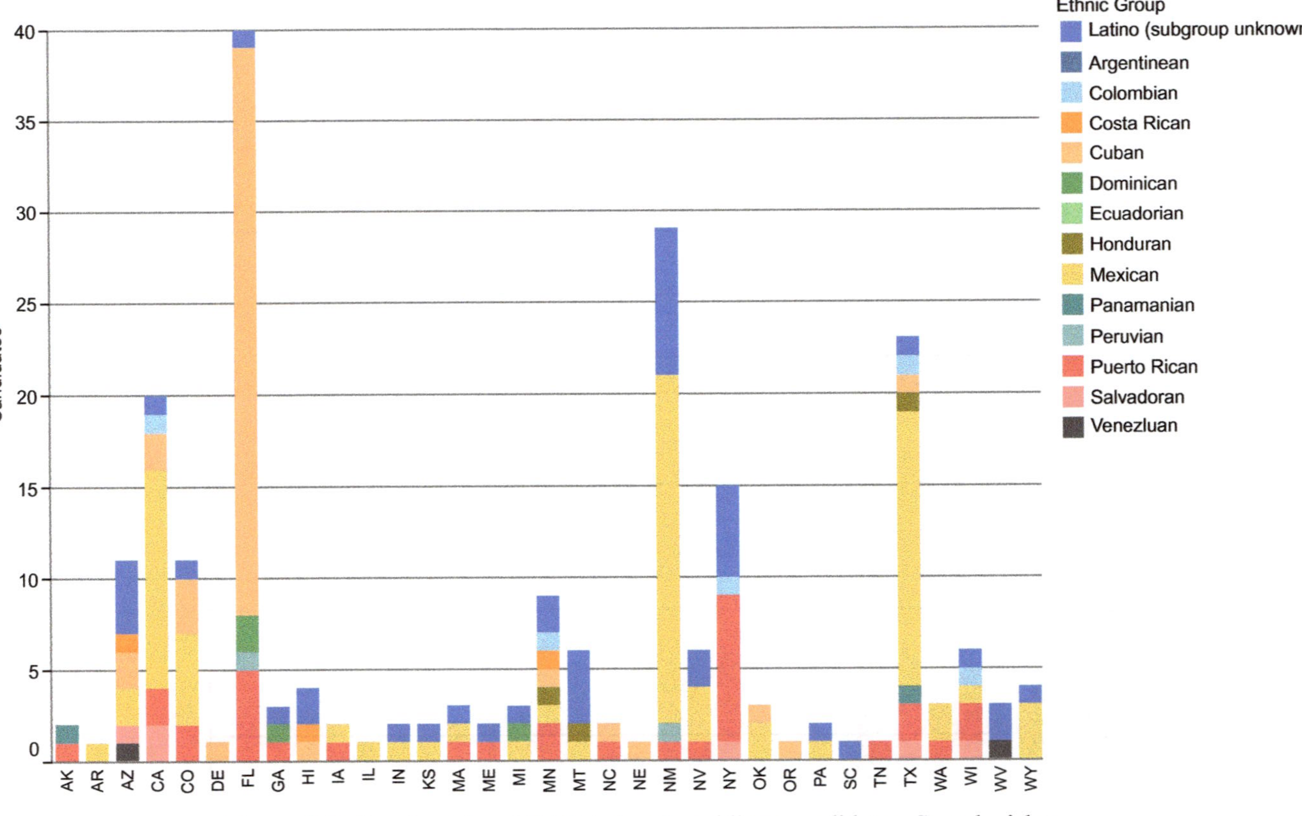

Figure 7 National origin of 2020 Latino Republican candidates: State legislature

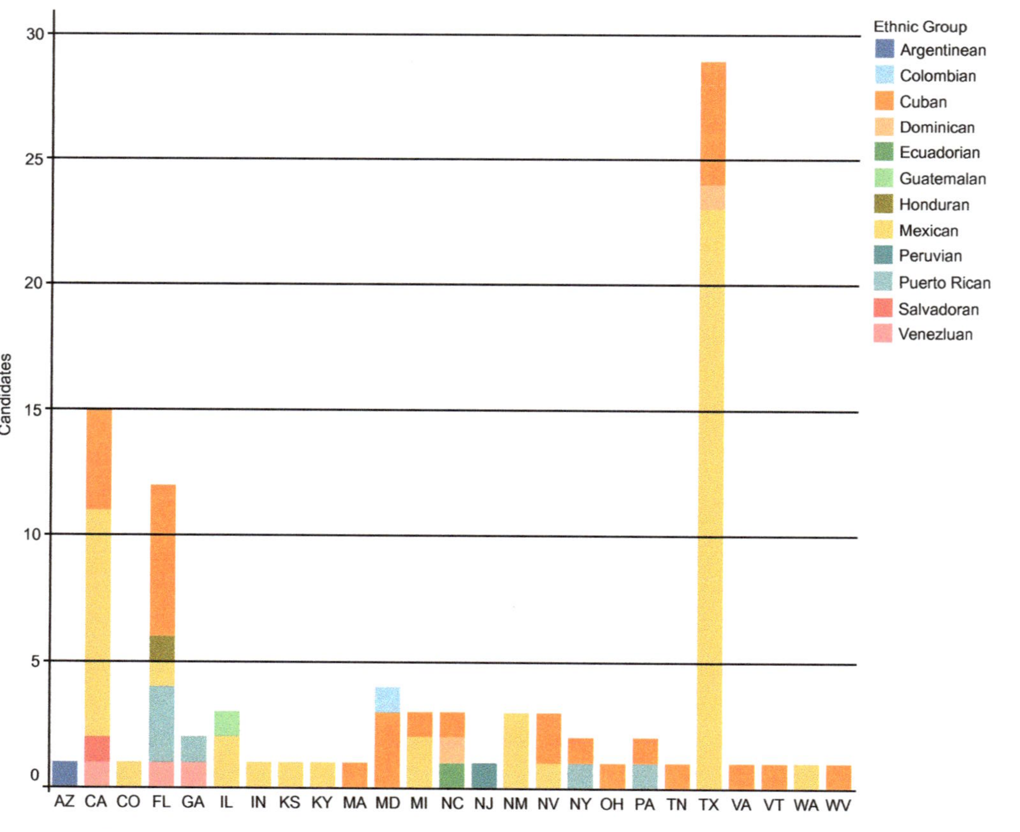

Figure 8 National origin of 2020 Latino Republican candidates: Congress

and 40 percent of Cuban candidates were women. Cubans also hold more congressional offices than any other Hispanic national origin group despite having fewer candidates than Mexicans. The regression analysis in Tables 8 and 9 shows,

Table 8 Hispanic origin groups of Latino Republican legislators

	Electoral Success
Argentinean	0.218
	(0.231)
Colombian	−0.082
	(0.209)
Costa Rican	−0.282
	(0.264)
Cuban	0.305[***]
	(0.096)
Dominican	−0.282
	(0.319)
Ecuadorian	0.218
	(0.319)
Honduran	−0.282
	(0.264)
Mexican	0.002
	(0.087)
Panamanian	−0.282
	(0.319)
Peruvian	0.718[**]
	(0.319)
Puerto Rican	−0.191[*]
	(0.104)
Salvadoran	−0.115
	(0.193)
Venezuelan	0.218
	(0.319)
Constant	0.282[***]
	(0.070)
N	223
R^2	0.158
Adjusted R^2	0.105
Residual Std. Error	0.440 (df = 209)
F Statistic	3.011[***] (df = 13; 209)

*$p < .1$; **$p < .05$; ***$p < .01$

Table 9 National origin groups of Latino Republican candidates for Congress

	Primary Election	General Election
	(1)	(2)
Cuban	0.333[*]	0.800[*]
	(0.190)	(0.418)
Mexican	0.413[**]	0.211
	(0.183)	(0.409)
Puerto Rican	0.500[*]	−0.000
	(0.257)	(0.460)
Salvadoran	1.000[*]	
	(0.505)	
Venezuelan	0.667[**]	−0.000
	(0.323)	(0.488)
Constant	−0.000	0.000
	(0.168)	(0.398)
N	94	35
R^2	0.090	0.397
Adjusted R^2	0.039	0.316
Residual Std. Error	0.477 (df = 88)	0.398 (df = 30)
F Statistic	1.746 (df = 5; 88)	4.930[***] (df = 4; 30)

*$p < .1$; **$p < .05$; ***$p < .01$

in line with our hypothesis, that Cubans are more likely to win in state legislative and congressional races than candidates of any other Hispanic origin group.

2.3.4 Latinas Surging

The increase of Latina candidates in 2020 from 2018 is perhaps the most significant of our findings. As Table 10 shows, the number of Latina candidates increased by over two and a half in 2020, rising from 23 percent of the candidate share to nearly 37 percent. At the congressional level, there was a similar increase from 16.6 percent to nearly 36 percent. Moreover, Latina candidates accounted for 70 percent of the total rise in Latino Republican candidates for Congress from 2018 to 2020.

As Figure 3 illustrated previously, the eighty-one Latina candidates are distributed all across the United States, which was not the case for the thirty-one who ran in 2018. Additionally, Latinas are represented by all but one of the recorded Latino national-origin groups. While our earlier discussion on the recent surge of Latina Republicans in Texas may partially explain our results, an increase of this

Table 10 Latino Republican candidates by gender

	Congress				State			
	Count 2018	Percentage of Latino Candidates (2018)	Count 2020	Percentage of Latino Candidates (2020)		Count 2018	Percentage of Latino Candidates (2018)	Count 2020	Percentage of Latino Candidates (2020)
Women	3	16.67%	10	35.71%	Women	31	23.13%	82	36.94%
Men	15	83.33%	18	64.29%	Men	103	76.87%	140	63.06%
Grand Total	18		28		Grand Total	134		222	

size suggests a more significant movement of Latina Republican politicians. These findings carry implications for the future of both the Latino electorate and the partisan balance of Latino politicians in the United States.

2.4 What These Findings Mean for Future Elections

The 2020 elections featured significant changes in the number, distribution, and ethnic backgrounds of Latino Republican candidates compared to 2018. While the number of Latino candidates in both parties increased, Republicans saw a much greater increase in their share of Latino candidates, nearly 10 percent at the state level and 13 percent at the congressional level. This, coupled with Latinos receiving a significant increase in candidates compared to other racial groups in the Republican Party, suggests that Latinos are making substantial in-roads with the Republican Party and vice versa, challenging the notion that Latinos are a monolith and highlighting the need for a better understanding of the Latino electorate and how it might influence future elections. To be sure, many of these Latino Republican candidates are running and winning in districts that are not majority-minority. Nevertheless, it is essential to ascertain where they are running, where they are winning, and what might contribute to these outcomes.

The geographic and ethnic distributions of 2020 Latino Republican candidates indicate a changing profile. While Texas, Florida, and New Mexico continued to see large candidate pools, Latino Republican candidates from multiple ethnic backgrounds are represented in thirty-three of the forty states covered in the 2020 C3 dataset. One possible explanation offered by extant literature and the media argues that Republican Party affiliation flourishes among immigrants from countries with a communist – or, by analogy, a socialist – government (Girard et al., 2012; Herrera, 2022). While this possibility could be a contributing factor, our findings show that many Latino Republican candidates are from countries that do not fit that bill. For example, this reasoning does not appear to apply in Montana, where the four (of six total) candidates with available ethnic background information were Mexican, Puerto Rican, Argentinean, and Honduran. Another explanatory factor is an increase in evangelical Latinos, which, as previously discussed, is associated with increased Republican partisan identification (American Trends Panel Wave 84, 2021; Navarro-Rivera, 2022). The possibility of religion informing these changes is worth further exploration as religious values are not subject to geographic constraints (in the United States) and often perform well in rural areas, allowing religious Latino Republican candidates the ability to campaign competitively in districts with religious constituencies, regardless of the Latino population in that district.

Our analysis of election outcomes carries similar implications. As previously alluded to in the discussion of our results, states with a high number of Latino Republican candidates in 2020, such as TX, AZ, NM, CO, and NY, saw few winners comparatively. In contrast, several states with low Latino populations, such as WY, MT, WV, PA, IN, and OK, all elected at least 50 percent of the candidates who ran. Much of the same is happening at the congressional level as well; while Texas, California, and Florida continue to lead the way, we are seeing a large increase in candidate interest in districts with low Latino populations. Some common themes shared by the campaign websites of these lawmakers in states with low Latino populations is that very few mention their Latino or national origin heritage, if at all, most highlight "good Christian values," and all focus on conservative values. The implication here is that Latino Republican candidates in largely non-Hispanic White areas are making the strategic decision to shift focus from their ethnicity, consistent with previous research showing this to be the case in the 2000s (Casellas, 2011b). In some ways, Latino Republicans in these majority White districts do not advertise themselves in terms of their Latino identity but rather focus on substantive representation of their constituents. At the same time, the national Republican Party touts its efforts to increase the number of Latino legislators nationwide (Contreras, 2022a). In what scholars have termed "symbolic" representation, a significant proportion of Latino GOP legislators are highlighted to help attract more Latino voters to the party, but at the same time, they are often representing districts with White majorities (Canon, 1999; Pitkin, 1967; RSLC, 2022a; Tate, 2001).

This trend poses significant challenges for political scientists because it makes classifying the ethnicity of Latino Republican candidates extremely difficult. Accurately determining ethnic origin required searching through thousands of candidates' personal social media sites, and even then, it is likely that several Latino candidates were missed and/or misattributed. If Latino Republican candidates are electorally incentivized to conceal their Latino heritage altogether, acquiring an accurate depiction of Latino representation at the state level might become quite challenging to ascertain.

The 2020 elections also saw a significant increase in the number of Latina Republican candidates at both the state and congressional levels, with Latinas seeing a similar geographic distribution to such candidates in general. Although the aforementioned implications apply to Latinos as well, the case of South Texas offers some insight into how Latina Republicans can achieve success. Are party elites trying to recruit Latinas to run, and if so, how does this vary by state? In the 2000s, some elites in the Republican Party actively recruited Latinos to run for office, but is that still the case given changes in who leads the Republican Party? (Casellas, 2011b)

In recent years, Texas has seen an emergence of Republican Latinas, both in voters and in candidates. Strong anti-communist rhetoric, meme-style attacks against Democrats, support of Trump, and prioritizing family values are among the tactics used by Latina Republicans in Texas that appear to be solid mobilizers for some Latino voters (Herrera, 2022). While it is unlikely that tactics such as these are solely responsible for the 2020 increase in Latina Republican candidates, further investigations into how this type of rhetoric resonates with the Latino electorate would likely offer insight into how and why Latinas are becoming more popular within the Republican Party. It also may be a larger Republican movement as 2020 saw more Women Republican candidates in general – although not to the same degree as Latinas.

The reach and diversity of Latino Republican candidates are much greater than previously anticipated and reflect a significant group that might influence future elections in many localities. In doing so, this section establishes the need for further monitoring of the Latino electorate, its power, how it can be harnessed, and how it is informed by religiosity, an important motivator often overlooked by political scientists. Furthermore, our findings suggest that where Latino Republican candidates run and how they choose to position themselves also deserve greater attention to more accurately determine Latino representation in the United States. Improved insight into these topics will allow us to better determine what factors are informing the increasing number of Latino Republican candidates. Equally important is how we choose to conceptualize representation, a topic that may see more relevance in the classification of candidates. Several Republican candidates were found to be Latino despite any campaign materials or biographical profiles pointing this out, indicating how some Latinos do not see themselves in racial or ethnic terms. These are all obstacles as Latino Republican candidates and the electorates they represent continue to evolve in ways that are often difficult to track and comprehend.

3 Latino Republican Legislator Ideology: More Conservative than White Republicans?

In the previous sections, we demonstrated the determinants of the election of Latino Republicans to state legislators and Congress after a comprehensive overview of the growth of these candidates running and winning across the country since 2018. These analyses gave us a better sense of the kinds of Latino Republicans who are getting elected nationwide. Unanswered, however, are the important questions regarding substantive representation, the extent to which the interests of Latinos are being represented (Casellas, 2011a; Pitkin, 1967). That is, do Latino Republicans vote differently than their non-Latino counterparts once in office? What are some of the factors that explain any differences or similarities of legislator ideology? Are there any differences by national origin group, gender, or district demography? This section will address these questions and conclude that Latino Republicans are generally more conservative than their non-Latino counterparts, Latina Republicans are more conservative than their male counterparts, and those representing majority White districts are the most conservative.

Using data on primary and general election candidates for state legislature and Congress from 2018 and 2020 in conjunction with district-level demographic data, this section further adds measures for legislator ideology to judge the efficacy of ideology as a predictor for Latino Republican electoral success. An added benefit of using legislator ideology is that it allows us to see how Latino Republicans differ ideologically from Republicans of other ethnicities. We conclude by discussing how ideology might make Latino Republican candidates more attractive and relatable to Republican voters in districts with low Hispanic populations.

Following our expectations laid out in the introduction, we test several hypotheses regarding the ideology of Latino Republicans. Our first hypothesis is grounded in the notion that Latino Republicans will be more ideologically conservative than non-Latino Republicans, given the widespread perception among White voters that Latinos are Democrats. Of course, this is a generalization, and in some places, such as South Florida, this perception is not apparent. In fact, historically, Cuban American Republicans in Congress have been less conservative than their White Republican counterparts when observing their DW-Nominate scores (Casellas, 2011b). However, this is starting to change as Republicans generally have become more conservative over time. Nevertheless, Latino Republicans often overcompensate for this perception by running and voting more conservatively than their non-Latino counterparts:

Latino Republicans Most Conservative *Hypothesis 1: Latino Republicans are more ideologically conservative on average than their non-Latino counterparts.*

Secondly, we believe that due to the gender gap and the presumption that Latinas are liberal Democrats, Latina Republicans exert even more of an effort to demonstrate their conservative credentials and run on and legislate much more conservatively than other Republican legislators and members of Congress. This has especially been the case in recent elections, with the ascent of prominent Latina Republicans in Congress, such as Anna Paulina Luna and Mayra Flores. Accordingly,

Latina Republicans Most Conservative *Hypothesis 2: Latinas are the most conservative subgroup of women among Republican state legislators and candidates for Congress.*

Given that Latino Republicans are often trying to appeal to White conservatives, we anticipate that as the proportion of Latinos in a district decreases, the more conservative Latino Republican legislators and members of Congress will be. Latino Republicans who represent majority Latino districts will be less conservative than those who represent majority White districts, as historically, this has been true even outside of South Florida. For example, Rep. Tony Gonzales of Texas represents a majority Latino district in South Texas and was challenged in the Republican primary in 2023 by Brandon Herrera, a YouTube influencer who gained notoriety by creating videos on guns. As such:

Majority White District Latino Republicans More Conservative *Hypothesis 3: Latino Republicans are more likely to be ideologically conservative as the proportion of Latinos living in a district decreases.*

Finally, we note that conservative Latino Republican candidates for Congress are much more successful as the proportion of Latinos in a district decreases. This is because these candidates make extra efforts to demonstrate their conservative credentials to a constituency that might assume otherwise. Therefore,

Latino Republican Conservative Candidates More Successful in Majority White Districts *Hypothesis 4: Ideologically conservative Latino Republican candidates for Congress see greater electoral success as the proportion of Latinos living in a district decreases.*

3.1 Measuring Ideology

To determine the ideological leaning of candidates for Congress, we use ideology measures from the Database on Ideology, Money in Politics, and Elections, also referred to as DIME scores (Bonica, 2023). The donation-based common-space DIME scores (CFscores) allow for direct distance comparisons of the ideal points of a wide range of political actors, including both members of Congress and congressional candidates. While we also collected DW-Nominate scores (Lewis et al., 2022) for members of Congress, this section primarily features DIME scores as the inclusion of candidates allows us to further explore the factors informing a surging candidate pool of Latino Republicans and identify trends that may not be observable with a sample that contains only elected officials. Furthermore, because DIME scores incorporate the source of campaign donations, they can convey how candidates are viewed ideologically rather than just depicting how they vote while in office. We believe this added versatility is well suited for analysis featuring congressional candidates, as those races increasingly have national implications and interests.

To gauge ideological differences among state legislators, we use 2020 individual legislator ideology scores taken from the Shor-McCarty individual state legislator ideology data set (Shor and McCarty, 2011, 2023).[1] The dataset uses a combination of archival and online data gathering in order to estimate ideal points of members of state legislatures from a large data set of roll-call votes cast between 1993 and 2023 (Shor and McCarty, 2011). These estimates summarize positions on large numbers of roll-call votes using a simple measurement model that lends itself to the statistical analyses below. The ideology scores allow us to illustrate how Latino Republican legislators differ ideologically from non-Latino Republican legislators. Moreover, the data also enables us to explore how legislator ideology varies across districts with different demographic characteristics.

To further elaborate on our choice of ideology measures, the complementary strengths and weaknesses of both DIME and roll call–based ideology scores are worth noting. DIME ideology scores, derived from campaign contributions, offer insights into how donors perceive candidates ideologically, allowing us to include both incumbents and challengers in our analysis. However, DIME scores may overemphasize the influence of donors and may not fully capture the policy positions of candidates who receive funding from ideologically diverse sources. This contrasts with roll call–based scores, which are calculated from actual legislative voting behavior and are limited to incumbents. While roll call scores directly reflect policy decisions made in office, they may obscure individual preferences due to party pressures on voting. Together, these measures provide different perspectives on ideological positioning, with DIME focusing on external perceptions and roll call capturing concrete legislative action.

Our analysis is divided into two sections addressing candidates for Congress and state legislatures, respectively. Each section uses a series of OLS regression models to gauge the ideological extremity of Latino Republican politicians. Additionally, we add two logistic regression models to our congressional ideology analyses to gauge how ideological extremity impacts election outcomes. We begin by comparing the ideology of Latino Republicans to their non-Latino counterparts before examining potential factors informing conservatism among Latino Republicans, such as the proportion of Latinos living within a district, gender, and incumbency status. These variables and our ideology measures allow us to both broadly and accurately illustrate the ideological positions that Latinos hold within the Republican Party.

---

[1] We also collected DIME scores for state legislators; however, DIME scores were only available for a small number of state legislators in our sample when compared to the coverage provided by the Shor-McCarty database. As such, this section features the latter.

3.2 Congressional Candidate Ideology

Building on our results from the previous section, Table 11 and Figure 9 show, consistent with our expectations, that Latino Republicans are among the most conservative candidates for Congress.

Black and Latino candidates are the only racial groups to exhibit a statistically significant relationship with ideological extremity, which may suggest that some minority candidates are being incentivized to ideological extremes to compete in congressional races. Indeed, some research on Black Republicans shows that, while often fairly conservative, they are less likely to become Republicans for a variety of reasons, including the role of linked fate and group consciousness (Philpot, 2017). However, the Black Republicans who run for Congress and make it there will be quite conservative. While White candidates have a positive relationship with ideological extremity, it is not statistically significant. Asian American candidates, on the other hand, tend to be less ideologically conservative than all other racial groups, and future comparative cross-ethnic research could explore some of the reasons why.

While Black candidates appear to be slightly more conservative than Latino candidates for Congress, that is not the case when we look at ideological

Table 11 Ideological extremity among Republican candidates for Congress

	Ideological Extremity
Latino	0.239^{**}
	(0.097)
Asian	-0.259
	(0.159)
Black	0.246^{**}
	(0.110)
White	0.126
	(0.091)
Constant	1.116^{***}
	(0.090)
N	444
R^2	0.048
Adjusted R^2	0.039
Residual Std. Error	0.323 (df = 439)
F Statistic	5.530^{***} (df = 4; 439)

$^*p < .1; ^{**}p < .05; ^{***}p < .01$

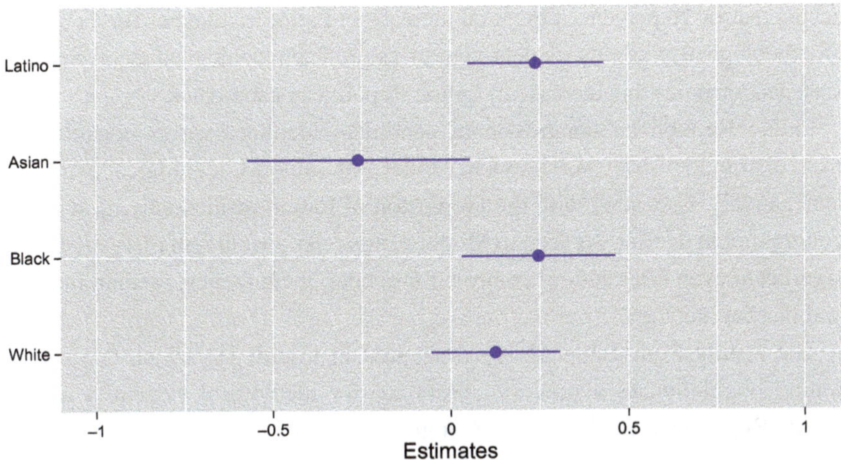

Figure 9 Ideological extremity among Republican candidates for Congress

Table 12 Ideological extremity among women Republican
candidates for Congress

	Ideological Extremity
Latina	0.416^{***}
	(0.155)
Asian	−0.249
	(0.233)
Black	0.158
	(0.168)
White	0.125
	(0.148)
Constant	1.197^{***}
	(0.143)
N	113
R^2	0.183
Adjusted R^2	0.153
Residual Std. Error	0.319 (df = 108)
F Statistic	6.053^{***} (df = 4; 108)

$^*p < .1; ^{**}p < .05; ^{***}p < .01$

extremity among Republican women running for Congress. Table 12 demonstrates that Latinas are most likely to be ideologically conservative by a considerable margin. As shown in Section 2, the number of Latina Republican candidates for Congress increased by over 230 percent from 2018 to 2020, and Latinas accounted for 70 percent of the total increase in Latino candidates for Congress. Our ideological extremity models suggest a significant ideologically conservative shift accompanies this increase in Latina Republican candidates.

Latino Republican congressional candidate ideology varies considerably from district to district. As shown in Model 1 of Table 13, ideological extremity is negatively associated with the proportion of Latino residents living within a congressional district. As seen in Model 2, this relationship remains statistically significant even after adding controls for gender, incumbency, median income, and district ideology.

The results from Table 13 are illustrated in Figure 10, which depicts the Latino population as a powerful predictor for ideological extremity among Latino Republican candidates for Congress.

The fact that candidate ideology becomes more conservative as the proportion of Latinos living in a district decreases is noteworthy, as it suggests that Latino Republicans are being incentivized to run in White-majority districts or are otherwise deciding to run in such districts, believing they have strong probabilities of winning.

Table 13 Determinants of ideological extremity among Latino Republican candidates for Congress

	Ideological Extremity	
	(1)	**(2)**
Latino Population	-0.584^{**}	-0.558^{*}
	(0.244)	(0.286)
Latina		0.060
		(0.136)
Incumbent		−0.133
		(0.306)
Median Income		0.000001
		(0.000004)
District Ideology		0.659
		(0.491)
Constant	1.723^{***}	1.672^{***}
	(0.112)	(0.351)
N	78	78
R^2	0.070	0.099
Adjusted R^2	0.058	0.037
Residual Std. Error	0.556 (df = 76)	0.562 (df = 72)
F Statistic	5.735^{**} (df = 1; 76)	1.590 (df = 5; 72)

$^{*}p < .1$; $^{**}p < .05$; $^{***}p < .01$

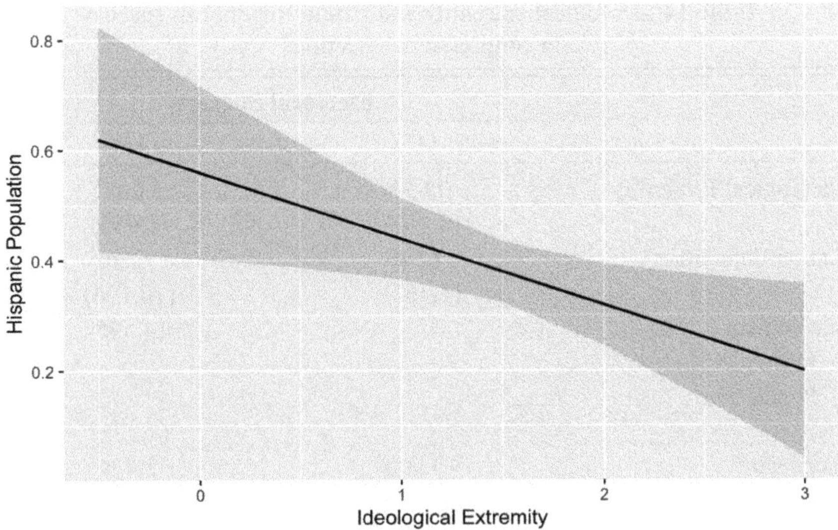

Figure 10 Latino Population and Latino Republican congressional candidate ideological extremity

As mentioned previously, one strength of the DIME ideology scores is that they also apply to candidates for Congress, which allows us to determine how ideological extremity affects the likelihood that a Latino Republican congressional candidate will win their election. Table 14 presents the results of two logistic regression models predicting Latino Republican candidate electoral success based on their ideological extremity and the proportion of Latinos living in the district they are running in. Model 2 adds an interaction between the two variables.

While neither variable in model 1 has a statistically significant relationship with electoral success, the results align with our theory that ideological extremity is positively associated with candidate success. In contrast, Latino population performs similarly to our results in Section 2, indicating a negative relationship with electoral success. Model 2, however, shows statistical significance across the board, with both Ideological extremity and the Latino population being associated with an increase in the log odds of electoral success when the corresponding variable is set to its reference level (zero). The interaction between ideological extremity and Latino population is noteworthy as it is the strongest predictor we test in terms of statistical significance, suggesting that the effect of a candidate's ideological extremity on their likelihood of winning is highly dependent on the proportion of Latinos living in their district, and will vary significantly as that proportion increases or decreases. This relationship is shown visually in Figure 11.

Table 14 Ideological extremity and Latino Republican success
in congressional elections

	Electoral Success	
	(1)	**(2)**
Ideological Extremity	0.654	3.602[*]
	(0.867)	(1.935)
Latino Population	−1.540	19.240[*]
	(1.462)	(10.196)
Ideological Extremity*Latino Population		−14.595[**]
		(7.222)
Constant	−0.990	−5.479[*]
	(1.521)	(2.889)
N	34	34
Log Likelihood	−20.940	−17.657
AIC	47.880	43.314

*$p < .1$; **$p < .05$; ***$p < .01$

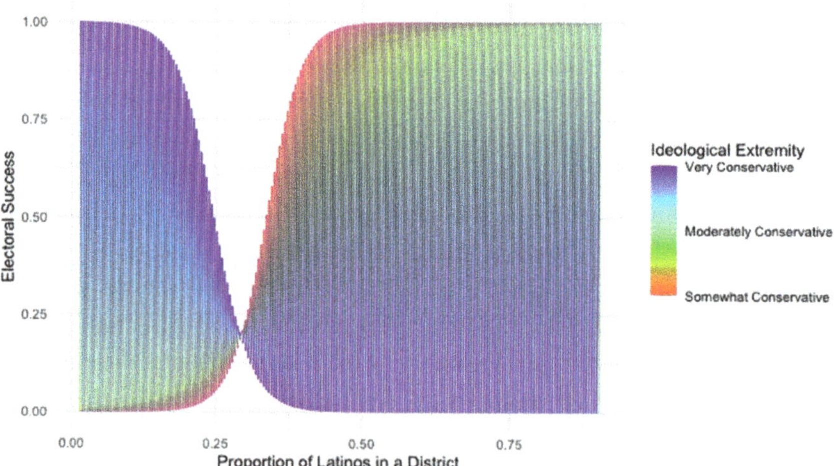

Figure 11 Predicted probability of electoral success by ideological extremity
and Latino population

As illustrated in the graph, ideological extremity's positive impact on winning decreases as the proportion of Latinos living within a district increases. The most conservative Latino Republicans see greater success in districts with low Latino populations, while candidates with low and moderate levels of conservatism see greater success in majority Latino districts. This finding is of great importance, as the results presented in this section and the following section suggest that Latino Republicans are among the *most conservative* candidates and legislators in the country at both the federal and state levels. Moreover, our findings from Section 2 indicate that while the number of Latino Republican candidates has increased significantly, this increase is being seen most prominently in districts with lower Latino populations. Taken together, the implication is a nationwide trend incentivizing Latino Republicans to run in non-Latino majority districts and often conceal or not emphasize their ethnicity during the campaign (Casellas, 2011b).

The relationships mentioned earlier are further fleshed out in our investigation into how ideology operates in state legislatures across the country, adding weight to the idea that the position and function of Latino politicians within the Republican Party is changing in ways that go beyond the dated notion that Latino Republicans were confined to South Florida and exclusively of Cuban origin.

3.3 State Legislative Ideology

While the results in the previous section show clear trends in Latino candidate success in state legislative districts with lower Latino populations, why this is occurring is less clear. Our analysis of ideology among Latino Republican state legislators may provide some clues. Table 15 shows, in line with our expectations, that Latino Republican state legislators are more conservative on average than non-Latino Republican state legislators, in addition to being the only racial/ethnic group among Republican state legislators to share a statistically significant relationship with ideological extremity.

The results of Table 15 are depicted in Figure 12, which illustrates the ideological distribution of Republican candidates by race. One key difference in our state-level analysis when compared to the congressional analysis is that Latino legislators are far and away the most conservative Republicans at the state level. In contrast, Black Republican candidates were slightly more conservative at the congressional level.

	Ideological Extremity
Latino	1.154[***]
	(0.129)
White	0.016
	(0.117)
Black	0.194
	(0.175)
Asian	−0.066
	(0.168)
Constant	0.903[***]
	(0.116)
N	2,159
R^2	0.161
Adjusted R^2	0.159
Residual Std. Error	0.436 (df = 2154)
F Statistic	103.366[***] (df = 4; 2154)

*$p < .1$; **$p < .05$; ***$p < .01$

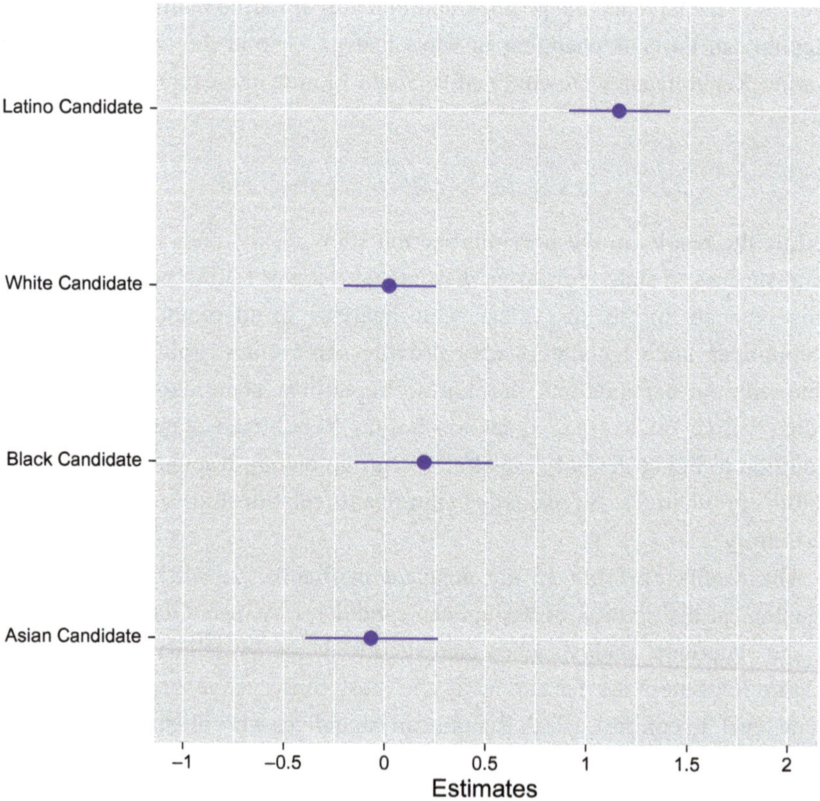

Figure 12 Ideological extremity among Republican state legislators

Table 16 Ideological extremity among women Republican state legislators

	Ideological Extremity
Latina	1.411***
	(0.328)
White	0.141
	(0.312)
Black	0.336
	(0.441)
Asian	0.002
	(0.369)
Constant	0.779**
	(0.312)
N	405
R^2	0.275
Adjusted R^2	0.268
Residual Std. Error	0.441 (df = 400)
F Statistic	37.968*** (df = 4; 400)

*$p < .1$; **$p < .05$; ***$p < .01$

When examining Republican state legislators, Latinos are the only ethnic group that appears to be a predictor of a conservative ideological extremity. These results are even more pronounced when looking specifically at Latina Republican state legislators. As depicted in Table 16, Latina legislators, like Latina congressional candidates, are much more likely to be ideologically conservative than their non-Latino counterparts. When considering these results in combination with the recent surge in Latina Republican candidates, it is apparent that the Latina candidate pool is rapidly changing. Previous research on Republican women shows that, in general, there are fewer Republican women in legislatures because they tend to be more moderate than their male counterparts, and there are fewer in the pipeline (Frederick, 2010; Thomsen, 2015). As partisan polarization increases, Latina Republicans are emerging to run and, compared to White Republican women, will often be more conservative and thus a better fit for Republican primary voters. However, as Wineinger (2022) shows, Republican women in general have become more conservative in recent years, contrasting to previous years when the Senate, for example, elected moderate Republican women from Maine, Kansas, and Texas (Swers, 2013).

Table 17 Determinants of ideological extremity among Latino Republican state legislators

	Ideological Extremity		
	(1)	**(2)**	**(3)**
Latino Population	-0.531^{**}	-0.431^{*}	-0.602^{**}
	(0.253)	(0.252)	(0.265)
Latina		0.307^{**}	0.304^{*}
		(0.152)	(0.157)
Incumbent			-0.159
			(0.150)
Upper Chamber			-0.066
			(0.159)
Median Income			-0.00001
			(0.00000)
Constant	2.333^{***}	2.201^{***}	2.865^{***}
	(0.107)	(0.123)	(0.374)
N	332	332	332
R^2	0.066	0.125	0.183
Adjusted R^2	0.051	0.096	0.112
Residual Std. Error	0.572 (df = 62)	0.558 (df = 61)	0.553 (df = 58)
F Statistic	4.396^{**}	4.362^{**}	2.595^{**}
	(df = 1; 62)	(df = 2; 61)	(df = 5; 58)

$^{*}p < .1$; $^{**}p < .05$; $^{***}p < .01$

To better contextualize these results, it is crucial to understand how ideology varies among Latino legislators. We examine these relationships in Table 17, which illustrates how the proportion of Latinos living within a district impacts Latino Republican legislator ideology before adding controls for legislator gender, incumbency status, upper/lower chamber status, and district median income.

The first finding of note is that the Latino population maintains a negative and statistically significant relationship with ideological extremity across all three models and with all controls, meaning that as the proportion of Latinos living in a district decreases, the conservative ideological extremity of Latino Republican legislators will increase (see Figure 13). While not statistically significant, incumbents and upper chamber seat holders appear slightly less extreme on average. Lastly, as seen with the congressional models, district income has little to no effect. The state-level ideological extremity models

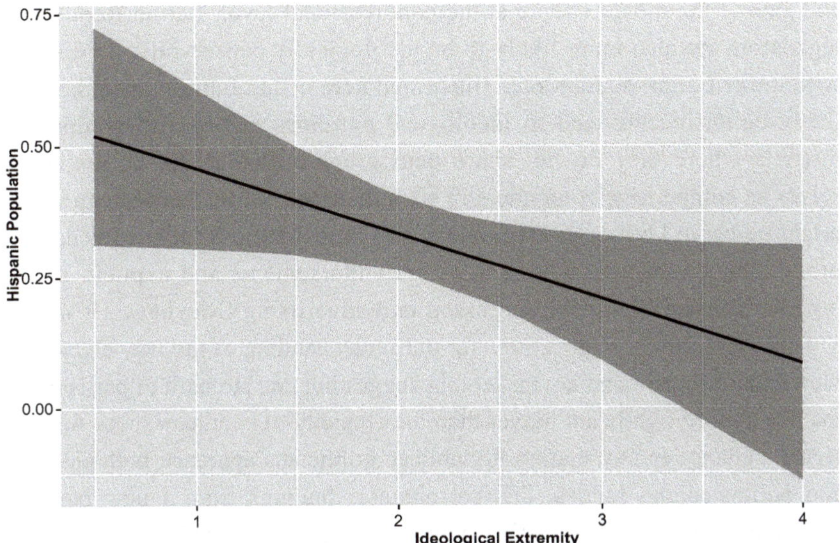

Figure 13 Latino population and Latino Republican state legislator
ideological extremity

perform in a very similar manner to our congressional models, suggesting a
national trend toward ideological conservatism among Latino Republicans at
the state and federal levels.

However, the most significant finding in Table 16 is the extent of Latina
Republican ideological extremity. In addition to being more ideologically
conservative than their male counterparts, Latinas are the most ideologically extreme Republican subgroup among state legislators measured in our
models. This shift toward conservatism among Latina Republicans,
coupled with the fact that much of the surge in Latino Republican candidates at the state and congressional levels consists of Latina candidates,
suggests that Latinas are central to the trend toward conservatism we are
seeing among Latino Republicans, especially in districts without Latino
majorities.

3.4 Understanding the New Normal

The findings of our legislator ideology models challenge previously held
notions of how Latinos operate within the Republican Party and offer
insight into how Latino Republicans are seeing success in districts with
lower Latino populations. Our models show that in addition to being the
most ideologically extreme subgroup among Republicans at the state level

and among the most extreme at the congressional level, Latino Republican legislators are also more likely to be ideologically conservative in districts with lower Latino populations. Illustrated here is that Latino lawmakers are likely being incentivized to ideological extremes in order to compete in districts where they do not share demographic similarities or see themselves as competitive contenders in such districts. White Republican voters might perceive Latinos as Democrats, and thus, Latino Republicans have to prove their conservative bona fides via endorsements and explicit, unambiguous conservative position-taking and advertising (Mayhew, 1974).

This trend carries implications for our understanding of the way electorates view Latino Republican lawmakers; in suggesting that strength of partisanship may be a more significant mover than the ethnicity of candidates, our findings signal a change in how Latino Republican politicians approach both elections and policymaking. Indeed, this corroborates findings from a new book by Grossmann and Hopkins (2024) demonstrating that Republicans are driven more by ideology than Democrats, who are driven by group representation. Republican voters are willing to support Latino candidates if they subscribe to conservative ideology. Previous work has shown that Whites, in general, would be less willing to support Black or Latino candidates due to racial resentment, but this explanation can only go so far and does not explain much of what we are observing with the growth of Latino Republicans elected from majority White districts.

If, as our findings illustrate, strength of partisanship is a more powerful mover than candidate ethnicity and Latino Republicans are incentivized to adopt ideological extremes to compete with their White Republican counterparts, then our results suggest this incentive is most evident among Latinas. Our findings indicate that Latina Republican candidates are becoming more conservative at a disproportionate rate when compared to male Latino politicians, a trend that is finding support through observable examples. Take, for instance, U. S. Representative Ana Paulina Luna of Florida. As one of the most conservative Latinas in the U.S. House, she first ran for Congress in 2022, endorsed by Donald Trump, Matt Gaetz, and Marjorie Taylor Greene. She authored a children's book suggesting that Joe Biden stole the 2020 election and has been outspoken in her view that the 2020 election was rigged. She did not begin identifying as Latina until 2019. According to news reports, in 2015, she ticked in her voting registration that she was "White, not of Hispanic origin." She was among a few House Republicans who did not support former Speaker Kevin McCarthy's multiple attempts to capture the speakership in January 2023. Examples like Luna's are emerging all across the American political landscape and further support the idea, reflected in our findings, that Latinas are emerging as the most conservative subgroup of Republican politicians.

Another relationship worth additional discussion is the finding that Latino Republicans become more conservative as the proportion of Latinos within a district *decreases*. There are likely several factors informing this relationship. As Section 2 addressed, outside of Latino-majority districts that are historically conservative in states like Texas, Florida, and California, among others, Latino Republican candidates are eschewing districts with high Latino populations in favor of majority White districts. This is, at least in part, a strategic decision, as most majority Latino districts outside of South Florida are historically Democratic strongholds. As such, Latino Republicans are targeting districts in which they stand a better chance of winning, where strength of partisanship is more salient among voters than a candidate's ethnicity (Juenke, 2014; Shah et al., 2022; Stout and Garcia, 2014). This is not to imply that ideological conservatism does not play well among Latino voters, as there is a growing body of research indicating that it does (Corral and Leal, 2024). Instead, it suggests that Latino Republican candidates are becoming more ideologically conservative in an attempt to level the playing field in districts where being Latino is not advantageous per se.

The added versatility of the DIME scores in our congressional ideology models allows us to measure how candidate ideology affects electoral success, furthering our understanding of the relationship between Latino population and Latino Republican ideology as a result. As the findings above illustrate, the chances of winning for ideologically conservative Latino congressional candidates dramatically increase as the proportion of Latinos living in a district lessens. To further contextualize these findings, it is worth noting that **most** Latino Republicans running in districts with a Latino population share of under 35 percent won in their general election, and the majority of Latino Republican candidates up for election in majority Latino districts were challenging incumbent Democrats, which again reinforces the idea that Latino Republican candidates may be making the strategic decision to prioritize their ideological leanings on the campaign trail rather than their ethnicity (Grossmann and Hopkins, 2024).

These nuanced dynamics reveal a strategic recalibration within the Republican Party, driven by Latino Republicans and magnified by the distinctive approach of Latina candidates. The trend toward greater conservatism among Latino Republicans, particularly in districts with a lower proportion of Latino voters, underscores a complex interplay between identity, ideology, and electoral strategy (Casellas, 2011a). This pattern suggests that Latino Republicans are not only navigating the political landscape with a keen awareness of demographic and ideological currents but are also actively shaping the contours of Republican Party politics. The success of Latino Republicans in majority White districts, bolstered by strong conservative credentials, points to a broader reconfiguration of electoral strategies that transcend traditional ethnic solidarity in favor of ideological alignment. This shift has profound implications for both the Republican Party's outreach efforts and the broader political representation of Latino communities in the United States.

In the coming electoral cycles, the ascent of ideologically conservative Latino Republicans, especially Latinas, challenges existing narratives about political alignment and party loyalty within Latino communities (Alvarez and García Bedolla, 2003; Barreto and Pedraza, 2009; Gimpel and Kaufmann, 2001; Hajnal and Lee, 2011; Saavedra Cisneros, 2016). It signals potential shifts in political engagement and policy priorities that could redefine Latino political identity in the coming years (Huddy et al., 2016; Sanchez and Masuoka, 2010; Stokes-Brown, 2012). These findings require further exploration into how Latino Republicans might influence the ideological spectrum of the Republican Party and the implications for Latino voter outreach and engagement strategies (Barreto, 2007; Corral and Leal, 2020; Mirilovic and Pollock III, 2018). As the American demographic landscape continues to evolve, the insights we gather from these trends will be crucial for understanding the future dynamics of American politics. The intersection of ethnicity, ideology, and electoral success not only offers a fertile ground for future research and political strategy but could also signal a significant moment of transformation within the Republican Party and the broader political sphere.

In the next section, we explore the cases of outliers, that is, Latino Republicans who are winning in majority Latino districts outside of South Florida. Fifteen years ago, the outliers would have been Latino candidates in general who were able to win in majority White districts, especially Democrats (Casellas, 2011b). However, as we have demonstrated, most Latino Republican candidates are running and successfully winning in majority White districts and majority Latino districts in South Florida; as a result, candidates winning in majority Latino districts have become the new outliers. In previously dominant Democratic areas of Texas and California, some Latino Republicans have been able to run and win, and the next section addresses these outliers, exploring who they are and how they are able to do it.

4 Explaining the "New Outliers": Who Are the Latino Republicans Winning in Majority Latino Districts?

So far, this Element has fundamentally reevaluated preconceived ideas about Latino Republican candidates by underscoring their expanding influence and diversity while establishing them as one of the most conservative elements within the Republican Party. As a result, our understanding of what constitutes an outlier among Latino Republican politicians must be updated in light of these dynamics. For decades, these outliers were the few Latino candidates of either party who won elections in majority White districts (Casellas, 2011a). The few Latino Republicans in office at the time were generally Cuban Americans representing South Florida districts.

Our data show that forty-six of the sixty-four Latino Republican state legislators in our 2020 dataset represent majority White districts, meaning that only 28 percent of Latino Republicans represent districts with a Latino majority. Our analysis at the congressional level tells a similar story, with only 18 percent of Latino Republican candidates running in majority Latino districts winning their general elections, compared to the 45 percent win rate of Latino Republicans running in majority White districts.

Another particularly noteworthy observation is that the few non-Cuban Latino Republican candidates who are winning in majority Latino districts are doing so in regions that are historically Democratic strongholds. This section aims to provide a deeper understanding of these new outliers by analyzing the sociopolitical dynamics that have enabled Latino Republicans to gain ground in traditionally Democratic, majority Latino districts. Through dissecting electoral and recruitment strategies, demographic shifts, and the broader national context, and by presenting detailed examples and case studies of notable candidates, we will illuminate the factors behind this political phenomenon. These illustrative cases will help contextualize the data-driven insights, offering a clearer view of the individual and collective paths these candidates have navigated. This investigation not only challenges traditional electoral narratives but also highlights a significant transformation in the landscape of American politics, where Latino Republicans are emerging as pivotal players in reshaping party alignments and voter base configurations in the United States.

In this section, we show that Latino Republicans are elected from majority Latino districts outside of Florida and are concentrated in California, Texas, and New Mexico. We argue that they do not necessarily tout their Latino identity, although some do, and they often are ideologically more conservative than Cuban Republicans from Florida. We call them outliers because it was not until relatively recently, with the growth of Latino Republican recruitment efforts, especially in Texas and, to a lesser degree, California, that these candidates began to run and win. To be sure, it is still the case that Democrats are more likely to win in majority Latino districts outside of South Florida, but this is beginning to change, and the rest of this section explains their ideology, issue priorities, and the extent to which they identify as Latino or provide Spanish-language communications.

4.1 Latino Republicans Winning in Majority Latino Districts outside of South Florida

As shown in Table 18, several Latino Republicans have been able to win in majority Latino districts outside of South Florida at the congressional level over the past few years. Consider the case of Monica de la Cruz of Brownsville, Texas. In 2022, the battle for Texas' 15th Congressional District between Republican Monica De La Cruz and Democrat Michelle Vallejo was among the state's most competitive House races, and De la Cruz's win helped establish Republican appeal among Latino Americans (Sanchez, 2022). She became the first woman and Republican to represent the 15th district of Texas since 1903, when she defeated Vallejo. An insurance agent, she decided to run for office in 2020 against incumbent Democrat Vicente Gonzalez, who defeated her that year. However, during redistricting, boundaries were shifted, and Gonzalez decided to run in a neighboring district, leaving the 15th district seat open. Unlike some of the other Latina Republicans profiled previously, De la Cruz

Table 18 Latino Republicans elected in majority Latino districts (U.S. House, 2022)

Name	State	Percentage of Latinos in District	Year Elected	National Origin Group	Ideology[a]
Mayra Flores	TX	90%	2022	Mexican	1.566
Monica De La Cruz	TX	81%	2022	Mexican	1.444
Maria Elvira Salazar	FL	74%	2020	Cuban	1.132
Carlos Gimenez	FL	73%	2020	Cuban	0.925
Mario Díaz-Balart	FL	73%	2002	Cuban	0.609
Mike Garcia	CA	65%	2020	Mexican	1.453
Tony Gonzales	TX	63%	2020	Mexican	1.406

[a] The ideology measurements listed in this table are DIME scores.

positioned herself as a more mainstream Republican by joining the Republican Main Street Partnership, a group of moderate Republicans in Congress. In describing her win, De la Cruz noted, "What we're seeing now is that the GOP has stepped in and helped us get our messaging out to show Latinos their values of faith, family, and freedom really align with the Republican Party." Her opponent, Vallejo, argued that the shift is tied to the GOP's increase in outside spending: "I think the resources and money they're getting from the outside really does add fuel to their fire … . It's not deeply connected with the desire from the community to drive up and bring solutions that are specifically from South Texas."

On her campaign website, De la Cruz touts that she is the first Latina and Republican to represent her district. She emphasizes her roots in Brownsville, where she was raised by a single mother, and her ties to other parts of the large district, which stretches from the border to the south of San Antonio. Her website has a Spanish-language link which appears to be directly translated from English. As we expected, her ideology score places her as the second most conservative Latino Republican in Congress, after Mayra Flores.

In addition to De la Cruz, Tony Gonzales also represents a majority Latino district in South Texas. He was first elected in 2020 when the 23rd district became open with the surprise retirement of Republican Will Hurd, the only Black Republican in Congress at the time who was considered a moderate in the party and briefly ran for president in 2023 on a conciliatory platform. Gonzales defeated Gina Ortiz Jones, a progressive Democrat, in 2020 and was reelected in 2022 by running on a moderate Republican platform. His voting record is similar to De la Cruz's in that Gonzales has gone against the party in several votes. In fact, he was censured by the Texas Republican Party for his votes in favor of LGBTQ rights and a gun safety bill passed in the aftermath of the Uvalde school shooting at Robb Elementary School. Gonzales faced YouTube influencer Brandon Herrera in the Republican primary, whose platform was that Gonzales was not sufficiently conservative, especially on gun control. Herrera was able to force Gonzales into a runoff, yet was defeated, buoyed by Gov. Greg Abbott's endorsement. Gonzales emphasizes on his website his experience in the U.S. Navy and the fact that his district shares 800 miles of the border with Mexico. In his section on immigration, Gonzales notes that he is a believer that "the American Dream does not always start in America" and emphasizes his support for fixing the broken immigration system. Gonzales has a Spanish-language website, which interestingly features a photograph with his wife with a different narrative of his background. The Spanish-language website discusses his foundation, which is aimed at helping economically impoverished neighborhoods in San Antonio. Gonzales represents a more competitive district than De la Cruz and is still a fairly conservative Latino Republican in Congress with an ideology score of 1.4,[2] placing him as more conservative than the Cuban Republicans from South Florida.

In California, Mike Garcia became the first Latino Republican to win in a majority Latino district outside of Florida in 2020. Representing the northern Los Angeles County suburbs, Garcia, like Gonzales, is a veteran of the U.S. Navy who served in the Iraq War and then worked for a defense contractor before running in the special election to replace Democratic Rep. Katie Hill, who resigned that year. Garcia was born in California to Mexican immigrants and positioned himself as a conservative in his run for office. His campaign webpage proclaims boldly, "I believe in capitalism," or alternatively, if refreshed, "I believe in the Constitution." His biography emphasizes his experience as a fighter pilot and identifies him as a first-generation American. Unlike Gonzales, there is no Spanish version or translation of his campaign website. Garcia is also fairly conservative, with an ideology score of 1.45, just slightly above Gonzales.

4.2 Latino Republican Success at the State Legislative Level

At the state legislative level, increasing numbers of Latino Republicans are running and winning in majority Latino districts, and New Mexico, as shown in Table 19, has the most significant number with seven representatives in their Legislature, three of whom are state senators. Following New Mexico is Texas, with four in their Legislature, one of whom is a state senator. In this section, we profile several of these Latino Republican legislators to highlight some of their similarities and differences.

In the case of State Representative Ryan Guillen of Rio Grande City, he started his political career as a Democrat. Like most Mexican Americans in South Texas, Guillen was raised in a community that has long been solidly Democratic. In 2002, at the age of twenty-four, he was elected to represent a largely rural majority Latino district that had long been represented by Democrats before him. As a state legislator, he was always among the most conservative Democrats, often voting with Republicans who have controlled the state legislature since the early 2000s. On issues such as abortion and gun control, Guillen's votes often aligned with Republicans despite his Democratic Party label.

---

[2] As noted in Section 3, we use different measures of ideology for Congress and state legislatures. As such, the scaling is different. For Congress, a score above 1.25 would be very conservative, whereas the threshold is a bit higher at the state level, around 1.7+.

Table 19 Latino Republicans elected in majority Latino districts (state legislatures, 2022)

Name	State	Percentage of Latinos in District	Chamber	Year Elected	National Origin Group	Ideology
Bryan Avila	FL	92%	House	2014	Cuban	1.67
Alex Rizo	FL	90%	House	2020	Cuban	2.144
Juan Fernandez-Barquin	FL	87%	House	2018	Cuban	2.045
Daniel Anthony Perez	FL	85%	House	2017	Cuban	1.692
Anthony Rodriguez	FL	84%	House	2018	Cuban	1.46
Tom Fabricio	FL	81%	House	2020	Cuban	2.174
Ryan Guillen	TX	72%	House	2002	Mexican	−0.425
Ileana Garcia	FL	72%	Senate	2020	Cuban	2.238
Demi Busatta Cabrera	FL	70%	House	2020	Cuban	1.653
Ana Maria Rodriguez	FL	69%	Senate	2020	Cuban	2.114
David Borrero	FL	68%	House	2020	Ecuadorian	1.854
David Gallegos	NM	67%	Senate	2020	Mexican	2.386
Peter Flores	TX	67%	Senate	2018	Mexican	2.856
Kelly K. Fajardo	NM	65%	House	2012	Mexican	1.565
JM Lozano	TX	64%	House	2011	Mexican	0.711
John Lujan	TX	64%	House	2021	Mexican	1.869

Table 19 (cont.)

Name	State	Percentage of Latinos in District	Chamber	Year Elected	National Origin Group	Ideology
Martin Ruben Zamora	NM	63%	House	2019	Mexican	2.25
Michele Pena	AZ	62%	House	2022	Mexican	NA
Gregory Baca	NM	61%	Senate	2017	Mexican	1.978
Luis Terrazas	NM	58%	House	2020	Mexican	1.8
Alonzo Baldonado	NM	57%	House	2011	Mexican	1.967
Rosilicie Ochoa Bogh	CA	44%	Senate	2020	Mexican	2.717
Joshua Sanchez	NM	42%	Senate	2020	Mexican	1.803

In 2021, Guillen decided to switch to the Republican Party. He became the first Republican at that point to represent his state legislative district. In describing why he switched parties, Guillen explained that "the ideology of defunding the police, of destroying the oil and gas industry and the chaos at our border is disastrous for those of us who live here in South Texas" (Svitek, 2021). The last Democrat prior to Guillen to switch parties in the Texas legislature was another South Texas Latino Democrat, J.M. Lozano of Kingsville, who switched in 2012. Democrats criticized Guillen for switching parties, noting that he was a political opportunist who became a Republican after the legislature made his district more Republican in the 2021 redistricting round. Of course, Guillen denied that this had anything to do with his decision, and with the endorsements of the House Speaker and Governor, Guillen went on to win the Republican primary and general election in 2022 by a comfortable margin. His district was one of several in South Texas carried by Donald Trump in the 2020 presidential election, which, albeit majority Latino, had become more supportive of Trump between 2016 and 2020.

On his campaign website, Guillen identifies as a sixth-generation South Texas rancher and small businessman. Proclaiming himself as "one of us," Guillen's website touts his legislative record, championing South Texas in the legislature and traditional conservative messaging. His campaign website does not appear to have a Spanish translation.

Guillen is not the only non-Cuban Latino Republican who was able to win a state legislative seat in a traditionally Democratic majority Latino area. In Arizona, Michele Pena ran for a Tucson area seat with no political experience and a paltry $1,600 budget in 2022. A single mother and school volunteer, she decided to run in the district adjacent to the border with Mexico. Her campaign was described as a grassroots effort with traditional outreach methods, including knocking on doors, Spanish-language advertisements, and emphasis on issues such as reducing inflation, improving education, and family values. During her campaign outreach efforts, she noted opposition from voters toward support of gender-neutral restrooms in schools (Reid, 2023).

Janie Lopez became the first Latina Republican to get elected in State House District 37 in South Texas in 2022. This district is in San Benito and includes Cameron County, adjacent to the border with Mexico, and has a Latino population of 83 percent. Her profile notes that her parents legally migrated from Mexico, and she identifies as a first-generation college graduate. Her platform is squarely in the conservative Republican mold, with photos of her and Governor Greg Abbott as well as highlighting her Christian beliefs. Her website indicates her issue priorities, with the first listed as "stopping transgender indoctrination in schools." Her website has an option for a Spanish translation, which does not deviate from the English version in terms of the biography and issue priorities.

Also from Texas, John Lujan was first elected in 2016 to represent State House District 118, which encompasses most of South and East San Antonio. The district is 63 percent Latino, and Lujan notes in his biography his twenty-five years as a firefighter in San Antonio and roots in the city where his father was a Protestant pastor. The top issue on his website is reducing property taxes, followed by public education and improving health care. His website does not have a Spanish translation. Lujan broke with his party several years ago by supporting Medicaid expansion (Svitek, 2022). Despite this, his ideology score is still fairly conservative, more so than that of his colleague Guillen.

In 2018, Pete Flores became the first Latino Republican to serve in the Texas Senate when he was elected in an open seat race to replace Democrat Carlos Uresti, who resigned after a corruption scandal. Flores was born in South Texas and emphasized his Texan roots in campaign materials prominently featuring him wearing a traditional cowboy hat. Prior to entering the Senate, he was a game warden with Texas Parks and Wildlife, and in his biography, he notes that he was the first Hispanic director of law enforcement for the agency. In 2020, he lost his senate seat to Roland Gutierrez, a Democrat who represented Uvalde, the town near San Antonio that was the site of a major school shooting at Robb Elementary. Gutierrez ran for the U.S. Senate in 2023 but lost the primary to Colin Allred, a congressman from the Dallas area. Texas GOP leaders drew a new district following the 2020 census to include Flores' town of Pleasanton and encompass much of former Sen. Dawn Buckingham's district, which she vacated to run for statewide office. Much in the same way in the past, elite-driven methods have helped Latinos win and attain office; Texas GOP leaders essentially created a new district for Flores, which he won comfortably in 2022, returning to the State Senate (Casellas, 2011a).

New Mexico also has a long tradition of Latino Republicans serving in office. While the state legislature has mostly been in Democratic control, Latino Republicans have made inroads in certain races. Take, for instance, Senator David Gallegos, representing the state's 41st district. Having first served on the school board in Eunice and then in the State House, he ran for State Senate in 2020 against an incumbent Republican and won on a conservative platform. The rural district in the southeastern part of the state is predominantly Latino but also mostly rural and conservative. While Gallegos does not have a Spanish translation on his website, his issue priorities listed are pro-life on abortion, support of the Second Amendment, and protecting the oil and gas industry.

Senator Gregory Baca, like some of the other Latino Republicans profiled earlier, served in the U.S. Navy, and when his service ended, he practiced law in Belen, a small town in New Mexico. In 2016, he defeated the Senate Democratic leader in this Belen-based district and became the Republican leader in the State Senate during his two terms in office. Because of redistricting controlled by the state's Democrats, Baca chose not to seek reelection in 2024. The new redistricting plan pitted two Latino Republicans against each other, and he decided to make way for his colleague (Brisbane, 2024).

Senator Joshua Sanchez is the other New Mexico Republican who was redistricted into the same district as Baca. Sanchez was also born in Belen and was first elected in 2020 to the 30th district, but after redistricting chose to run in Baca's 29th district, which included both of their constituencies. His website notes his issue priorities of crime, jobs, and infrastructure, and touts his legislative accomplishments, including a $50 million hospital facility in his district. His campaign website does not appear to have a Spanish translation or make note of his ancestry.

In terms of ideology, as shown in Table 19, Gallegos is the most conservative of the three New Mexico senators, and his district has the highest percentage of Latinos. The least conservative is Sanchez, whose district is 42 percent Latino, suggesting that some of these rural majority Latino districts, not only in Texas but also in New Mexico, are electing Latino Republicans who are quite conservative and do not seem too moderate to appeal to a Latino constituency.

4.3 Broader Implications for American Politics

The trends highlighted, particularly those showing Latino Republicans winning in historically Democratic, majority Latino districts, carry several significant implications for the Republican Party. First, Republicans are expanding their outreach efforts into new territories and making efforts to appeal to historically Democratic Latinos. Some appeals, no doubt, capitalize on efforts by some progressive Democrats to emphasize cultural issues such as transgender rights, abortion rights, LGBTQ acceptance, and efforts to use the term Latinx. For example, a 2024 Pew Hispanic Survey shows that only 4 percent of Latinos use the term to describe themselves (Noe-Bustamante et al., 2022). Success in these districts suggests that the GOP can potentially expand its electoral map into areas previously considered strongholds of the Democratic Party. This could alter strategic resource allocation in future elections, pushing the Democratic Party to invest more heavily in Latino-majority areas.

As our research has shown, with Latino Republican candidates, the GOP can make gains in states that are critical in presidential elections, such as Arizona and Nevada. Should the GOP see more success in majority or plurality Latino districts, it might continue to highlight aspects of its platform that align with the conservative values prevalent among many Latino voters, such as family, entrepreneurship, the economy, and religious freedom. While a reassessment of party issue positions on immigration policy, for example, might not be required to gain a foothold in these districts, it may help in retaining these districts long term. It is important to note that, in recent election cycles, the GOP's stance on immigration, as embodied by Donald Trump, has not harmed them in many of the Latino majority districts we analyzed earlier. While counterintuitive to some, there has always been a significant percentage of the Latino population with conservative, restrictionist views on immigration and support Republicans not despite these positions but because of them.

4.4 Latino Republican Success in Majority White Districts and States

While the previous sections of this section have addressed the outliers in our data, which are Latino Republicans winning in majority Latino districts, it is important that we also say more about Latino Republican success in majority White districts. Although Latino Republican success in White districts is not a new phenomenon, these successes used to be the outliers until recently when it became the norm (Casellas, 2011a). How are Latino Republicans performing so well with White voters? There is a commonly held misperception that race and ethnicity are among the most powerful predictors of vote choice. This, however, is not the case, as a growing body of research has shown that ideology and partisanship are far more powerful movers among voters (Westwood et al., 2018).

One reason for this is that who a person chooses to support politically is a personal decision, whereas factors like race and ethnicity are assigned at birth (although ethnicity can be a choice). As such, because one's partisanship is often a deliberate decision for an individual, it is considered a choice that more accurately reflects who that person truly is (Martinovich, 2017). Another reason is that, unlike race, religion, and gender, where social norms dictate behavior, there are few limitations on the expression of hostility toward people who support opposing political ideologies (Westwood et al., 2018). Certain boundaries will always apply when speaking on race/ethnicity and religion. For the most part, few boundaries exist in a partisan environment, especially considering that party elites often encourage hostility (Westwood et al., 2018).

This research is further supported by a recent Harvard poll that finds political ideology to be a much more powerful predictor of both vote choice and political attitudes than gender, race, ethnicity, and religion (Harvard-IOP, 2024). When looking specifically at White Americans, it has long been established that White racial identity can predict their sociopolitical attitudes and behaviors. However, when it comes to predicting support for political candidates, it remains an unclarified question whether the effects of White identity politics are determined more by candidates' ideology or race (Jardina, 2019).

Research published in 2021 finds that ideological leaning is more predictive of candidate support than race/ethnicity across four separate studies and shows that conservative White Americans support the most conservative candidate more often than not, regardless of the candidate's race or gender (Bai, 2021). The explanatory power of ideology as a predictor for candidate support is noteworthy when considering that Section 3 established Latino Republicans as among the most conservative subgroups in American politics, a finding that helps explain why Latino Republicans are beginning to see increased success in White districts. Another factor to consider is that candidates may be intentionally concealing their Latino heritage in their campaign materials or choose not to emphasize or make policy proposals based on their ethnic background.

In Ohio, however, Trump endorsed car dealership owner Bernie Moreno, who won the Republican nomination for U.S. Senate to challenge incumbent Democratic Senator Sherrod Brown in 2024. Moreno has not shied away from identifying as a first-generation immigrant born in Bogota, Colombia. His website's first sentence in the "About me" section indicates this. His campaign emphasized the American Dream and his success as an entrepreneur in Ohio having made his fortune selling cars. In a 2016 interview with Global Cleveland, Moreno notes that immigrants should be welcomed, "otherwise it is not America," and stressed the importance of legal immigration (Global Cleveland, 2016). His 2024 campaign website has a list of policy priorities, and securing America's borders is listed second behind advocacy of school choice. While his website does not include a Spanish translation, this might have more to do with Ohio's demographics, which only has a 4 percent Latino population. Moreno won the Republican primary by garnering Trump's endorsement and, despite Republican governor Mike DeWine's endorsement of his opponent, a more mainstream Republican. In the campaign, Senator Brown pointed to Moreno's life story as disingenuous in that he comes from a well-connected and influential family in Colombia, defying the rags-to-riches message of his campaign. Moreno's parents earned graduate degrees from the University of Pennsylvania and Stanford, respectively, and his brother served as Colombia's ambassador to the United States.

4.5 Evolving Dynamics of Latino Republican Representation

It was not very long ago that the only Latino Republicans elected from majority Latino districts were Cuban Americans in South Florida. Outside of these outliers, the vast majority of Latino elected officials were Democrats. To be sure, there were pockets of Republicans elected in New Mexico and Texas, but by and large, areas with denser concentrations of Latino residents would elect Democratic representatives. As shown in Casellas (2011b), however, there were ideological differences between Democrats elected from cities in the Northeast and rural areas in the Southwest. Then Representative James Taylor, a Democrat from New Mexico, identified himself at the time as a "New Mexico Democrat," which he defined as having conservative positions on some of the social issues such as abortion and gun rights. In the same way many White conservative Southerners gradually shifted to become Republicans, we are beginning to see this happen in the rural areas of Texas, Nevada, and, to a lesser extent, California. While not as dramatic as the political realignment of the American South in the 1990s, we are witnessing shifts primarily driven by rural, evangelical, working-class Latinos who have been receptive to Republican appeals.

This section has given a more in-depth look at the Latino Republicans outside of South Florida who have been able to win in majority Latino districts. They are the new outliers in that they have overcome the odds to win in places that have not historically elected Republicans. They have many things in common, but also adjust their strategies to appeal to their constituents. At the congressional level, Texas has seen the emergence of two conservative Latina Republicans representing swaths of South Texas along the border. Monica de la Cruz has compiled a fairly conservative voting record but, at the same time, emphasizes her Latina heritage and Spanish-language communications. On the other hand, her colleague Tony Gonzales, representing another district in South Texas, has compiled an even more moderate Republican voting record, leading to a primary challenge from the right. This suggests that all politics is local, and even in South Texas, there are differences between the Republican members of Congress.

At the state legislative level, we show that more Latino Republicans have won in majority Latino districts, mainly in Texas and New Mexico. Arizona has also seen one candidate win, but the multi-member district method of electing legislators there entails only thirty districts statewide, with voters choosing two lower chamber members and one upper chamber member from one district. If Arizona had a more traditional single-member district system with smaller House districts and larger Senate districts, it would probably be the case that there would be more Latinos in general in the State House and possibly more Latino Republicans.

As more candidates are bound to run for office in these areas, future research can seek to understand in more detail how Latino Republicans are able to be successful in these districts and test hypotheses as more data is collected and trends are identified. In particular, this section has highlighted that in terms of ideology, Latino Republicans from majority Latino districts are often fairly conservative, often more so than the South Florida legacy Cuban Republicans. This in and of itself suggests that the conventional wisdom that Cubans are the most conservative Latinos might not be the case anymore. Party identification is more entrenched in Cuban American circles so that even though the ideology of Cuban representatives has shifted left (albeit still very much to the right of Democrats), more Latino Republicans are emphasizing conservative values in districts that have always identified that way ideologically but not Republican. For Latinos in these areas, ideology and partisanship are not as correlated as for White Americans. This is seeming to change at the moment in South Texas and other rural parts of the Southwest as many Latinos are beginning to sort themselves into the more conservative party.

Moreover, we observe variance in the extent to which Latino Republicans elected in these districts emphasize their Latino heritage and/or Spanish language. Some officials have Spanish websites and communicate with their constituents this way. Others do not have Spanish websites and do not seem to prioritize this. In the future, a more systematic analysis of Spanish-language communications and/or analysis of communication of Latino identity could identify ways in which different legislators view their roles in representing people of Latino backgrounds.

In the next section, we conclude by identifying our major contributions in this Element and how scholars, policymakers, and political operatives should reflect on how the nation's largest minority group is beginning to exert more influence in one of the two major political parties, and how these trends might affect American politics in the years to come.

5 Conclusion: The Changing Face of Latino Political Representation

Thus far, this Element has provided a comprehensive examination of the evolution of Latino Republican representation in the United States, highlighting a significant shift in the political landscape. Our findings demonstrate that the reach, diversity, and ideological conservatism of Latino Republican candidates have grown considerably. This transformation is not merely a statistical anomaly but reflects a broader trend that could reshape future elections and alter our understanding of Latino political representation.

In Section 2, we documented the expanding influence and diversity of Latino Republicans, showing that they are no longer confined to traditional strongholds such as South Florida and Texas. Instead, they are emerging in unexpected regions, gaining traction in both state legislatures and Congress. This diversification includes a broader array of national origin groups, gender representation, and increasing geographic distribution. Notably, Latina Republicans have shown a remarkable increase in their numbers and are among the most conservative members of the party.

Second, in Section 3, we revealed that Latino Republicans are generally more ideologically conservative than their non-Latino counterparts. This ideological shift is particularly pronounced among those representing majority White districts, indicating a strategic adaptation to appeal to conservative constituencies more broadly. The data suggests that as the proportion of Latinos in a district decreases, the conservatism of Latino Republican candidates increases, highlighting apparent efforts to align more closely with the core values of the Republican base.

Section 4 highlighted the emergence of "new outliers," Latino Republicans winning in majority Latino districts traditionally held by Democrats. These candidates often leverage conservative values and strategic campaigning to appeal to a constituency that has historically aligned with the Democratic Party. This phenomenon underscores the growing ideological diversity within Latino Republican ranks and suggests that Latino Republicans can be competitive even in areas that have not traditionally supported the Republican Party. The success of these candidates challenges the conventional wisdom about Latino voting behavior and indicates a potential shift in the political allegiance of Latino voters. Moreover, Section 4 also addressed the success of Latino Republicans in majority White districts and the implications of these victories, examining how ideological alignment and strategic campaigning have enabled these candidates to overcome historical barriers and discussing the consequences of these trends for the future of Latino representation in American politics.

The rest of this section will explore several key relationships associated with the rise of Latino Republican candidates, as well as the implications shaped by this surge and its impact on American politics. We will identify various factors, including Republican outreach strategies, targeted recruitment of Latino candidates, and shifts in Latino voter dynamics. Additionally, we will address how our findings fit into the literature on Latino representation and the implications of these trends for the future of American politics.

We begin by examining the Republican Party's strategic outreach efforts over the course of the twenty-first century, which have played a crucial role in identifying and supporting Latino candidates. This includes establishing initiatives such as the Right Leaders Network and the Future Majority Project, aimed at fostering a diverse pool of candidates. Next, we analyze the shifts in Latino voter dynamics that have contributed to this shift. Factors such as economic concerns, cultural issues, and conservative values have resonated with a growing segment of the Latino electorate, leading to increased support for Republican candidates and possible challenges for the Democratic Party in maintaining its traditional Latino voter base.

By synthesizing these insights, we aim to provide a nuanced understanding of the evolving political landscape and the factors driving the rise of Latino Republicans. This conclusion offers a comprehensive overview of how these trends will likely shape future elections, what this means for both major political parties in the United States, and how the findings discussed in this Element add to our understanding of an essential feature of American politics.

5.1 Republican Outreach Strategies

In 2012, the *Texas Tribune* covered increased Latino outreach efforts by the GOP headed by George P. Bush and Steve Munisteri, who started a project to identify GOP-leaning Latinos in Texas by cross-referencing consumer data and voter rolls to find conservative Latinos who they could recruit as Republican voters (Root, 2012). It was thought that the compassionate conservativism of George W. Bush, George P. Bush's uncle, is what helped him perform much stronger with Latinos than previous Republicans who were historically perceived as the party of the rich. Bush's more tempered discourse on immigration, Spanish-language appeals, and advocacy of educational reforms were thought to be the perfect recipe for Latino outreach (Wroe, 2008). Once Bush left the political scene, Republican presidential nominees John McCain in 2008 and Mitt Romney in 2012 failed to capitalize on Bush's efforts, and the Latino vote reverted to levels seen in the Clinton years, with Republicans capturing between 25 and 28 percent of the Latino vote in the presidential elections.

Despite these lackluster performances and Obama's ability to forge and maintain a winning coalition, Republicans continued efforts during the Obama years, building a bench of their candidates nationwide and focused efforts on capturing statehouses. Indeed, during the Obama years, Republicans managed to make significant gains in seats at the state legislative level, and this included many Latinos (Grumbach, 2022). At the 2012 Republican National Convention, George P. Bush said: "We're rolling up our sleeves and doing the dirty work in Hispanic outreach, and we're going to be collaborating with the Republican Party helping to identify, recruit and support qualified candidates to go run for office." These efforts continued despite the party's lurch rightward on many issues, especially immigration, most notably in states with large Latino populations. For instance, in 2012, the Texas GOP hired a fluent Spanish speaker, David Zapata, as its minority outreach coordinator, a first for the party in that state (Root, 2012).

Officials in Texas also conducted outreach to increase the number of Latino delegates to their convention, and about 700 of the 9,000 delegates to the state convention in Fort Worth were of Latino descent. Four of the 24 new members of the State Republican Executive Committee were also Latino (Root, 2012). These efforts in Texas have contributed to making it more difficult for Democrats to make inroads in a state that has long been seen as a place where Democrats would benefit from growth in the Latino population in a hope that demography is destiny, but scholars Corral and Leal (2024) have called this hope "el cuento del destino," an assumption that should be reconsidered in light of empirical evidence to the contrary.

Despite some perceptions that the nomination of Donald Trump would be a death knell to Latino outreach efforts, the Republican Party has continued to invest in outreach and has yielded some dividends despite the incredulity of many who cannot conceive that Latinos would support the party of Trump. Several Republican leaders in states across the United States rolled out ad campaigns intended to target prospective Latino candidates in the 2020 and 2022 election cycles (Contreras, 2022a). The Republican State Legislative Committee (RSLC), which supports down-ballot state legislative and state-level offices, has invested in its first Spanish-language ad and has more than sixteen Latino candidates in its "Right Leaders Network" recruitment and training program, including in New Mexico, Texas, California, Florida, Oregon, and Illinois (RSLC, 2022b). Most recently, it announced that it would be working with Texas House Speaker Dade Phelan (R) to fund a $360,000 ad buy to support two Republican candidates in Texas: Reps. Janie Lopez in the Rio Grande Valley and John Lujan in San Antonio.

These efforts add to GOP hopes of boosting the party by making inroads in Latino communities, which has been a major focus of national Republican leaders. This is in addition to other groups investing in Latino communities, such as the Libre initiative, a group promoting free market principles in Latino neighborhoods.

In 2022, the Republican National Committee set up twelve Hispanic community centers where staff worked to build relationships and outreach and launched a program to help immigrants prepare for their naturalization tests (Lonas, 2022). While since their initial establishment, many of these centers have closed, some analysts such as Daniel Garza of the Libre Initiative noted, "In this case they went big and it sounds like they didn't get the response from the community they intended" (Carrasquillo, 2024). It remains to be seen if and how the RNC will resurrect some of these centers.

The National Republican Congressional Committee has increased its Latino candidate recruitment efforts in the 2024 electoral cycle, and the party is generally bullish about its prospects with Latino voters, a group that has become an increasingly important part of the Democratic coalition. Their optimism stems from decades of success pursuing Florida Latino voters but also from recent key electoral wins elsewhere, particularly in South Texas. However, the Democratic Party and the Biden campaign made efforts in April 2024 to appeal to Latino voters. Biden appeared in a lengthy sit-down interview with Spanish-language television station Univision and invested in advertisements on ESPN Deportes and La Liga, making efforts to reach out to working-class Latino men, a group that Republicans are targeting (Ward, 2024). When Biden stepped down in July 2024, Vice President Kamala Harris adapted her Latino outreach strategy by focusing less on identity politics and more on issue-based appeals focused on the economy, high drug prices, and crime. Harris visited the border and promised to crack down on illegal immigration and the smuggling of fentanyl across the border (Messerly and Diaz, 2024).

5.2 Latino Republican Candidate Recruitment

The Republican Party's efforts to recruit Latino candidates began taking shape during the George W. Bush presidency and continued into the Obama era. This early groundwork, which included initiatives like the Future Majority Project and outreach efforts targeting Latino voters in states such as Texas, laid the foundation for the surge in Latino Republican candidates seen in the elections examined in previous sections. While the party's Latino candidate recruitment efforts have increased significantly since 2020, these efforts, which we detail in this section, represent a continuation and expansion of earlier efforts rather than their inception.

Recently, Republicans have been quick to build a steady bench of Latino candidates, focusing on economic issues and traditional family values, while Latino Democrats had to struggle within their party for years to grow their numbers, relying on natural candidate emergence rather than specific targeting and funding of promising candidates. To be sure, there are candidate training programs that target Democrats, such as Emily's List and the Victory Fund, but it was not until very recently that the Latino Victory Project, a progressive campaign group, established a program targeted at finding and recruiting prospective Democratic candidates to run for office in key states such as Arizona, Pennsylvania, Texas, and Wisconsin (Bernal, 2023).

The GOP has also worked on appealing to groups beyond their Cuban American base. They have been ramping up efforts to recruit Puerto Rican candidates and voters since the 2016 election cycle (Salomon and Torrens, 2018). The results of these efforts are reflected in our data, as the number of GOP candidates who identify as Puerto Rican has increased dramatically since 2018. This is especially the case in the Orlando area of Florida, an important swing region in the state.

To be clear, Latino Democrats in Congress outnumber Republicans four to one, but the Republican Party has recruited a new generation of Latino candidates at breakneck speed, most notably in Texas but also in states like Oregon and Virginia. The National Republican Congressional Committee reported that it recruited a total of 102 Latino candidates in the 2022 cycle (Bernal, 2023). Many of these candidates are women, who have been shown to be more electable than men (Bejarano, 2014).

This concerted effort to recruit Latina candidates has focused on targeting prospective individuals from state legislatures, law schools, and various business communities. The recruitment efforts have been strategic, with bases of operation being set up in high-leverage locations with high Latino populations, such as Southern California, South Florida, and South Texas (Cohen, 2023; Zhou, 2022). According to Fernand Amandi, president of Miami-based research and strategic communications at the Democratic consulting firm Bendixen & Amandi, "the GOP has excelled at managing the margins. Part of that strategy is recruiting and running Hispanic candidates, especially Latinas, to try and pick off a point or two here and there, which in some states and in some races represents the very margin between victory and defeat" (Cohen, 2023). As shown in previous sections, Republicans have been able to flip long-held Democratic majority Latino districts in large part because of the aforementioned targeted recruitment efforts.

The GOP has laid the foundation for becoming more diverse since 2012 (Zhou, 2022). After losing the presidential election in 2012 – when candidate Mitt Romney won just 30 percent of Latino voters – the Republican National Committee commissioned a postmortem report. It concluded that the RNC needed to "make certain that we are actively engaging women and minorities in our efforts" when it came to candidate recruitment and that "we need to strengthen our farm team to ensure that we are competitive in up-ballot elections in the future when the electorate will be considerably more diverse." The idea was that electing a more representative pool of officials to state and local office could help Republicans reach a broader base of voters and establish a deep bench for federal seats down the line. That RNC report boosted efforts like the Republican State Leadership Committee's "Future Majority Project," which is dedicated to identifying and backing women and people of color for Republican seats at the state level. The project had some success, including wins by 43 of 240 recruits in 2014.

Additionally, a number of emerging PACs targeting Latina Republican candidates have worked to make inroads in areas not historically associated with Latino Republicans.

Since 2018, House Republicans have increased their number of Latino members to over 50 after concerted recruitment efforts and a slew of wins by Latino candidates from Oregon to Texas to Virginia (Mutnik, 2022). In fact, "this year's [2022] recruits span nearly every region of the country and range from Brazilian to Mexican to Guatemalan descent" (Mutnik, 2022). Former House Speaker Kevin McCarthy credited Latino candidate recruitment efforts, particularly those targeting Latinas, as one of the key factors that delivered the House to the Republicans in 2022 (Lonas, 2022; Zhou, 2022).

The fact that Latino Republican midterm contenders delivered big wins for the GOP without moderating their MAGA identity is cause for alarm among Democratic leaders. As noted earlier, the Kamala Harris campaign shifted its Latino outreach efforts to focus less on ethnic-based appeals and more on the economy, even hardening her position on immigration.

5.3 Shifts in Latino Voter Dynamics

The surge in Latino Republican candidates since 2018 has been accompanied by noticeable shifts in Latino voter dynamics. These changes are not just reactions to recent electoral cycles but are closely tied to the increasing visibility and outreach efforts of Latino Republican candidates. As more Latino Republicans emerge, the ideological landscape within Latino communities should continue to change, reflecting the broader appeal of the GOP to segments of the Latino electorate. And while the so-called red wave never came to pass in 2022, there was nevertheless a noticeable shift among Latino voters in the midterms, who still tilted toward Democrats overall but reached higher levels of Republican support than in 2020 (Martinez, 2023a).

According to data released by the Pew Hispanic Center, 39 percent of Latino voters supported Republicans in the 2022 midterms, compared to 25 percent in the 2018 midterms (Hartig, 2023). Republican gains among Latino voters occurred in a year when former President Trump was not on the ballot, though many candidates he endorsed were (Martinez, 2023b). While more Latinos continue to favor the Democratic Party, their allegiance is shifting. Many Latinos have signaled growing differences on cultural issues, crime, and the economy, giving Republicans hope that they might have an edge (Contreras,

2023b). Ipsos pollster and senior vice president Chris Jackson put it this way: "Latinos are still more Democratic than Republican by significant margins, but when you're talking about elections that are won by a percentage point, small losses can make a difference." In states such as Arizona, where President Biden carried by 10,000 votes in the 2020 election, these types of shifts can make a huge difference in who is elected president.

These shifts to Republicans did not begin in 2022, as Trump's performance among Latino voters improved greatly in 2020 compared to 2016, despite his loss to President Biden overall (Fraga et al., 2025). In Florida, Trump won half the Latino vote, surging among Republican-leaning Cuban Americans, Puerto Ricans, and other Latinos, especially Venezuelans (Teixeira, 2023). But contrary to early reports that these shifts were only noted in South Florida and South Texas, Trump improved his performance among Latinos by 20 points in Wisconsin, 18 points in Texas and Nevada, 12 points in Pennsylvania and Arizona, and among urban Latinos in Chicago, New York, and Houston. In Chicago's predominantly Latino precincts, Trump improved his raw vote by 45 percent over 2016 (Teixeira, 2023).

Trump's success with Latinos extended far past urban centers, with Latinos voting for Trump in smaller, historically Democratic towns, such as Reading, Pennsylvania, just outside of Philadelphia (Zitner, 2021). Furthermore, data from Catalist, a progressive data firm, confirm a nationwide shift to Republicans among Latinos in 2020. The Democrats' overall margin among this group dropped by 18 points relative to 2016. Cubans had the largest shift of 26 points, but Puerto Ricans moved by 18 points to Trump, Dominicans by 16 points, and Mexicans by 12 points. An overall weak spot for Democrats was among Latino men, who gave Trump 44 percent of their two-party vote in 2020 (Teixeira, 2023).

In 2022, while Democrats did not lose much more ground, they did not gain any back either. Since the 2022 midterm election, polls have consistently found that Latino voters prefer Republicans to Democrats on inflation and handling the economy, and in a recent *Washington Post*-ABC News poll, Latinos preferred the way Trump handled the economy when he was in office to Biden's performance so far by 55 to 36 percent (Teixeira, 2023). Data released by the Gallup Organization in 2024 shows that Democrats' longtime advantage with Black, Latino, and Asian American voters has shrunk to its lowest point in more than sixty years, creating vulnerability for Democrats (Contreras, 2024). Notwithstanding criticisms of some of these polls based on small sample sizes or different weighting schemes, these findings are noteworthy, as they signal that one of the most loyal parts of the Democratic coalition is possibly in play. Blacks and Latinos could vote Republican in numbers not seen since President

Dwight D. Eisenhower was elected in the 1950s, further complicating hopes for Democrats to control Congress and the presidency (Contreras, 2024). At the same time, no Republican presidential candidate has won the popular vote since George W. Bush's reelection in 2004, giving Republicans their own complications in forging a winning coalition.

Even still, this drop-off in Democratic support comes after many members of the party's leadership predicted for years that racial and ethnic demographic shifts would give Democrats a political majority for decades (Judis and Teixeira, 2002). Republican consultant Mike Madrid believes that these predictions are based on the assumption that Latinos are predominantly civil rights voters, stating "that not all people of color have deep ties to the Civil Rights Movement" and that "the Latino population was small during the Civil Rights era. Today, few children of immigrants who came after the 1960s know who civil rights leaders Gus Garcia, Héctor P. García, or Dolores Huerta are." Sisto Abeyta, a Democratic political consultant in New Mexico, warned that if Democrats want to continue to count on Latino voters, they need to make a massive shift in their messages, stressing that Democrats' focus on abortion rights and the environment is not appealing to some Latinos, as the face of abortion tends to be White women and climate change fights are reduced to just purchasing an electric vehicle (Contreras, 2024). Furthermore, there is a growing consensus that identity politics do not play well with many Latinos (Campero, 2020). These shifts have not only changed the electoral landscape but also created opportunities for Latino Republican candidates to position themselves as advocates for values and policies that resonate with a significant number of Latino voters.

A closer look at Latino voter dynamics in New Mexico helps to illustrate why Latinos are beginning to shift away from Democrats. New Mexico has long been the most Latino state in terms of the share of the state population and has had a long tradition of Latino representation in its legislature and delegation to Congress (Casellas, 2011a, 2011b; Vigil, 1996). It is a majority Latino state and has had Latino governors of both parties in recent years. Latino ranchers and farmers in northern New Mexico whose families have been in the region for centuries say they are losing confidence in Democrats over policies they say hurt their way of life because Democrats have shaped their agenda around White and Latino college-educated voters (Contreras, 2023a). Specifically, some of these farmers report that Democrats' positions on protecting endangered species ignore their reality and long fights with the federal government. For example, protections for the meadow jumping mouse and the Mexican gray wolf mean the ranchers' grazing and water rights are limited on their land, directly affecting their livelihoods. David Sanchez, a rancher in Monero, NM, said some longtime Latino ranching Democrats are considering voting for Republicans because they are less aggressive about forest regulations and give more attention to rural areas because Democrats seem too focused on climate policies developed by people who have never lived in rural areas or electric vehicles, which currently are not feasible in vast regions like northern New Mexico (Contreras, 2023a).

Many ranchers live on lands given to families by the Spanish crown during colonial times (Gutiérrez, 1987). The 1848 Treaty of Guadalupe Hidalgo, which ended the U.S.-Mexico War, promised the United States would honor the land grants and rules around them, such as access to grazing, water, and land ownership. Indeed, in the 1960s, New Mexican civil rights leader Reies Lopes Tijerina grounded his activism precisely on the failure of the United States to recognize these promises. The Latino ranchers say the United States has ignored and violated the treaty – including by limiting land rights through conservation efforts – amid years of discrimination. Carlos Salazar, a rancher in Medanales, New Mexico, says that when former President "Trump was in office, we had four peaceful years in the allotments." Trump rarely interfered with ranchers' rights or imposed new regulations (Contreras, 2023a).

Recent election cycles in South Texas show that the Latino vote is not a monolith, and parties that treat it that way do so at their own risk. Nonetheless, Republican and Democratic candidates alike have targeted Latino voters as a key demographic they hope to win over since 2022. And for good reason: Latino Texans are now the largest demographic group in Texas and one of the fastest growing (Despart and Svitek, 2022).

South Texas also shows the differences in how each party approaches Latino voters. Banking on an identity-based appeal, Democrats focus on the sort of bilingual messaging in South Texas that has played well among Mexican Americans in Los Angeles and Puerto Ricans in New York, focused on a celebration of diversity and immigration. Republicans, by contrast, recognized that Latino South Texans share many of the same values as non-Latino White voters elsewhere in Texas and swept in with a pitch about defending gun rights, promoting the oil and gas industry, restricting abortion, and supporting law enforcement (Herrera, 2021). For decades, the dominant ideologies in South Texas have been the same as in other rural areas and small towns across the state – that is, conservative. Moreover, many Latino South Texans shared something else with non-Hispanic White rural Texans: their racial identity. Latino residents in Texas are much more likely to identify as White than Latino residents of cities elsewhere in the country (Herrera, 2021).

The GOP has looked at South Texas and sees many voters who walk and talk like Republicans. The challenge facing the Democratic Party is not just how to win back Latino voters. It is how to win back voters with Latino names who may not even use that adjective to describe themselves. These trends show no signs of slowing down (Cadava, 2022). While Democrats have historically won the majority of Latino votes in presidential elections, that margin has been narrowing since 2016 (Cadava, 2022). Spring 2024 polling by *The New York Times* showed Trump with a 6-point lead among Latino voters, a significant shift since Joe Biden won 60 percent of their votes in 2020 (Medina, 2024). Regardless of the accuracy of this particular poll, given small sample sizes or other methodological shortcomings, it should be a wake-up call to Democrats. According to Maria Echaveste, a senior policy official during the Clinton administration and Mi Familia Vota board member, this shift reflects the increasing generational and ethnic diversity within American Latino communities (Baker, 2024). She added that "Democrats have very incorrectly assumed that Latinos only care about immigration. And that's just not true, most are more concerned about jobs, taxes and the economy when it's time to vote."

This is important, as Latinos made up approximately 15 percent of all eligible voters during the 2024 presidential election but have often been overlooked or written off in recent years, having been erroneously considered a monolithic voting bloc.

When considering the findings in this Element, coupled with identifiable trends in Latino voter preferences, the evidence suggests a mutual influence where the presence of more Latino Republican candidates may be affecting the ideological landscape. This potential feedback loop, where increased visibility and outreach efforts by Latino Republican candidates both reflect and contribute to changes in voter behavior, warrants further investigation. We hope Latino politics scholars will further explore these dynamics to better understand the implications for future elections and Latino political representation.

5.4 Situating Our Findings

The findings and contributions of this Element have broad implications for the future of Latino representation and American politics as a whole. By situating our analysis within the broader literature on Latino representation, we can better understand the significance of the recent trends and what they mean for future elections.

The evolution of Latino Republican representation, as documented in this Element, aligns with the growing body of research that highlights the increasing diversity and political engagement within Latino communities. Studies have long noted the potential for Latino voters to significantly influence American elections due to their rapid population growth and geographic dispersion

(Casellas, 2011b; Fraga et al., 2010). Our findings build on this literature by providing empirical evidence of how Latino Republicans have capitalized on this potential, diversifying their reach and ideological stance.

In highlighting the expanding influence and diversity of Latino Republicans, we demonstrated their emergence beyond traditional strongholds like South Florida and Texas. This reflects broader demographic shifts and supports the argument that Latino political engagement is becoming more geographically widespread and varied (Hero and Preuhs, 2013). The increase in Latina Republicans, noted for their significant conservatism, underscores the importance of gender dynamics within Latino political representation, building on literature that explores the intersectionality of race, gender, and political ideology (Bejarano, 2014).

Latino Republicans are generally more ideologically conservative than their non-Latino counterparts, particularly in majority White districts, suggesting that minority candidates are incentivized to adopt more extreme positions to counteract stereotypes and appeal to broader conservative constituencies. The ideological shift among Latino Republican candidates suggests a strategic adaptation that resonates with the broader electorate. This could represent a type of political assimilation in which minority candidates align their ideologies with the dominant party's values to gain acceptance and electoral success.

Our focus on the "new outliers" – Latino Republicans winning in majority Latino districts traditionally held by Democrats – challenges conventional wisdom about Latino voting behavior and could be the beginning of a more significant trend that should be further explored. This phenomenon underscores the growing ideological diversity within Latino Republican ranks and suggests a potential realignment of Latino political allegiances. This supports literature that questions the monolithic portrayal of Latino voters and highlights their complex and evolving political identities (Greene and Kim, 2019; Stokes-Brown, 2018).

5.5 Looking to the Future: Implications for American Politics

Our findings suggest several key implications for future elections. The first is that the increasing ideological conservatism among Latino Republicans, especially in majority White districts, indicates that the Republican Party's outreach and recruitment strategies have been effective. This trend will likely persist as the GOP continues to diversify its candidate pool and appeal to Latino voters through targeted messaging on economic and cultural issues.

These strategic decisions by Republicans have left the Democratic Party facing significant challenges in retaining Latino support. The perceived disconnect between the national party's priorities and the concerns of Latino voters, particularly those related to economic issues and cultural conservatism, could lead to further erosion of their traditional Latino voter base (Gallup, 2024). Democrats must address these concerns by broadening their appeal and enhancing their engagement with Latino communities to remain competitive. Some candidates, such as former Rep. Ruben Gallego of Arizona —now a U.S. Senator— have made efforts to specifically target working-class Latino men, demonstrating their ability to win over Latino voters in contrast to Biden (Collins, 2024). To be clear, the kinds of issues that appeal to Latinos in Alexandra Ocasio-Cortez's New York City district will not be the same in Vicente Gonzalez's South Texas valley district. Both are Democrats, but Republicans are only posing a threat to the South Texas Democrats at the moment due to the perceived disconnect between national Democrats and rural Texas Democrats.

Moreover, the Democratic Party's emphasis on social issues like abortion rights and LGBTQ+ advocacy may not appeal as strongly to many culturally conservative Latinos, especially in regions like South Texas, where traditional values hold sway even in historically blue districts (McNamee, 2022; UnidosUS, 2023). The party's challenge is to address these concerns more effectively and counter the perception that it takes Latino votes for granted. Some Latino voters feel that Democrats assume their loyalty without sufficiently engaging with their communities or addressing their specific issues (González, 2024).

The success of Latino Republicans in traditionally Democratic strongholds suggests a potential shift in political allegiances. As Latino voters become more ideologically diverse, both parties will need to adapt their strategies to address the nuanced priorities of this electorate. This includes recognizing the importance of economic stability, public safety, and educational opportunities, as well as respecting cultural values and identities.

When taken together, the broader implications for American politics include a more competitive and unpredictable electoral landscape. As Latino representation within the Republican Party grows and diversifies, we can expect to see more Latino candidates influencing policy and shaping the party's future direction. Increased representation also means that Latino voters will have a more significant impact on election outcomes, making their support crucial for any winning coalition. With this in mind, future research should continue to explore the dynamics of Latino political representation, focusing on the long-term impact of these trends on American politics. This includes examining the effectiveness of different outreach strategies and the evolving priorities of Latino voters.

The rise of Latino Republicans and the shifting dynamics within Latino voter behavior marks a pivotal change in American politics. Both major political parties can develop more effective and nuanced strategies to engage with Latino communities and address their diverse concerns by understanding these trends and their implications. The future of Latino representation in American politics will likely be characterized by greater ideological diversity and increased political engagement, shaping the landscape of future elections and policy decisions.

References

Abrajano MA and Alvarez RM (2012) *New Faces, New Voices: The Hispanic Electorate in America*. Princeton, NJ: Princeton University Press.

Alberta T (2022) Why Democrats Are Losing Hispanic Voters – The Atlantic. www.theatlantic.com/politics/archive/2022/11/hispanic-voters-fleeing-democratic-party/671851/ (accessed May 14, 2024).

Alvarez RM and García Bedolla L (2003) The foundations of Latino voter partisanship: Evidence from the 2000 election. *Journal of Politics* 65(1). Chinese Corporation for Promotion of Humanities: 31–49.

Bai H (2021) Politicians' ideology matters more than their race in determining the association between white identity and evaluation of the politicians. *Social Psychological and Personality Science*. https://doi.org/10.1177/19485506211039396. 13(5). Los Angeles, CA: SAGE: 978–993.

Baker K (2024) Latino Voters Are Swinging Back toward Trump and the GOP. https://thefulcrum.us/ethics-leadership/donald-trump-latino-voters (accessed April 26, 2024).

Ballotpedia (n.d.) California State Senate District 23. https://ballotpedia.org/California_State_Senate_District_23.

Barreto MA (2007) ¡Sí Se Puede! Latino Candidates and the Mobilization of Latino Voters. *The American Political Science Review* 101(3). Washington, DC: Cambridge University Press: 425–441.

Barreto MA and Pedraza FI (2009) The renewal and persistence of group identification in American politics. *Electoral Studies* 28: 595–605.

Barreto M and Segura GM (2014) *Latino America: How America's Most Dynamic Population Is Poised to Transform the Politics of the Nation*. New York: Public Affairs.

Bedolla LG (2014) Latino Politics, 2nd Ed. *eTextbooks for Students*. Epub ahead of print 1 January.

Bejarano CE (2013) *The Latina Advantage: Gender, Race, and Political Success*. Austin, TX: University of Texas Press: 1–183.

Bejarano CE (2014) *The Latino Gender Gap in U.S. Politics*. New York, NY: Routledge. www.routledge.com/The-Latino-Gender-Gap-in-US-Politics/Bejarano/p/book/9781138903104 (accessed May 14, 2024).

Bernal R (2023) Latino Victory Project Names New Leadership. www.aol.com/latino-victory-project-names-leadership-144940670.html (accessed May 19, 2024).

Bishin BG and Klofstad CA (2009) Author's personal copy Deceit, diversity, or mobilization? Intra-ethnic diversity and changing patterns in Florida's Hispanic Vote. *The Social Science Journal* 46: 571–583.

Bishin BG and Klofstad CA (2011) The political incorporation of Cuban Americans. *Political Research Quarterly*, http://dx.doi.org/10.1177/1065912911414589. 65(3). Los Angeles, CA: SAGE: 586–599. https://journals.sagepub.com/doi/10.1177/1065912911414589 (May 19, 2024).

Bonica A (2023) Database on Ideology, Money in Politics, and Elections (DIME). https://doi.org/10.7910/DVN/O5PX0B.

Bowler S and Segura GM (2012) *The Future Is Ours: Minority Politics, Political Behavior, and the Multiracial Era of American Politics.* Thousand Oaks, CA: CQ Press.

Bratton KA and Haynie KL (1999) Agenda setting and legislative success in state legislatures: The effects of gender and race. *Journal of Politics* 61(3). Chinese Corporation for Promotion of Humanities: 658–679.

Brisbane J (2024) Sen. Greg Baca Not Seeking Reelection. www.koat.com/article/sen-greg-baca-not-seeking-reelection/60182114 (accessed May 18, 2024).

Cadava GL (2020) *The Hispanic Republican: The Shaping of an American Political Identity, from Nixon to Trump.* New York City, NY: Harper Collins.

Cadava G (2022) The Democratic Party's Latino Voter Problem. www.nytimes.com/2022/01/18/opinion/democratic-party-latino-voters.html (accessed April 26, 2024).

Callister AH, Galbraith Q, and Galbraith S (2019) Immigration, deportation, and discrimination: Hispanic political opinion since the election of Donald Trump. *Hispanic Journal of Behavioral Sciences* 41(2). SAGE: 166–184.

Campero M (2020) Identity Politics Do Not Play Well with Latinos. *Center for Strategic & International Studies.* www.csis.org/analysis/identity-politics-do-not-play-well-latinos.

Canon DT (1999) *Race, Redistricting, and Representation: The Unintended Consequences of Black Majority Districts.* Chicago, IL: University of Chicago Press: 324.

Carrasquillo A (2024) The RNC Shuttered Most of the Hispanic Community Centers It Touted as Critical to Winning over Latino Voters (Exclusive). https://authory.com/AdrianCarrasquillo/The-RNC-Shuttered-Most-of-the-Hispanic-Community-Centers-It-Touted-as-Critical-to-Winning-Over-Latino-Voters-Exclusive-ae7c8b124feae47e282d8575826cda66d (accessed May 19, 2024).

Casellas JP (2011a) Latinas in legislatures the conditions and strategies of political incorporation. *Aztlán: A Journal of Chicano Studies* 36(1): 171–189.

Casellas JP (2011b) *Latino Representation in State Houses and Congress.* Cambridge: Cambridge University Press. www.cambridge.org/core/books/ latino-representation-in-state-houses-and-congress/E0894D9EB7E2E298A8B D84764D7085CD.

Caygle H (2017) Hispanic Caucus denies membership to Republican Curbelo – POLITICO. www.politico.com/story/2017/11/16/congressional-hispanic- caucus-deny-carlos-curbelo-244977 (accessed May 19, 2024).

Chong D and Kim D (2006) The experiences and effects of economic status among racial and ethnic minorities. *American Political Science Review* 100(3). Cambridge University Press: 335–351.

Cohen Z (2023) Latina Candidates Courted by GOP to Diversify House Majority | Bloomberg Government. https://about.bgov.com/news/latina-can didates-courted-by-gop-to-diversify-house-majority/ (accessed April 16, 2024).

Collins E (2024) In the Arizona Senate Race, Ruben Gallego Shows Democrats What It Takes to Win Back Latinos – WSJ. www.wsj.com/politics/elections/ arizona-senate-race-latino-voters-gallego-lake-a6a8b9b7 (accessed May 19, 2024).

Combs MW, Hibbing JR, and Welch S (1984) Black Constituents and Congressional Roll Call Votes. *Political Research Quarterly* 37(3). SAGE: 424–434.

Contreras R (2022a) GOP Pushing Hispanic State Legislator Candidates to Flip Dem Seats. www.axios.com/2022/08/11/hispanic-republican-legislators (accessed August 28, 2022).

Contreras R (2022b) Record Number of Hispanic Republicans Run for New Mexico House Seats. www.axios.com/2022/04/19/record-number-hispanic- republicans-new-mexico (accessed August 28, 2022).

Contreras R (2023a) A Small Group of Ranchers Helps Illustrate Latinos' Shift away from Democrats. www.axios.com/2023/07/27/rural-hispanic-voters- ranchers-yellowstone-democrats (accessed April 26, 2024).

Contreras R (2023b) Latinos Slowly Drifting from Democrats, Exclusive Poll Shows. www.axios.com/2023/06/22/latino-drift-democrats-poll (accessed April 26, 2024).

Contreras Russel (2024) Why Democrats Are Losing Black, Hispanic Voters to the Right. www.axios.com/2024/03/13/why-democrats-black-hispanic-vote- republican (accessed April 26, 2024).

Contreras Russell (2024) Why Democrats Are Losing Black, Hispanic Voters to the Right. www.axios.com/2024/03/13/why-democrats-black-hispanic-vote- republican# (accessed May 14, 2024).

Corral ÁJ and Leal DL (2020) Latinos for Trump? Latinos and the 2016 presidential election. *Social Science Quarterly* 101(3): 1115–1131.

Corral ÁJ and Leal DL (2024) El Cuento del Destino: Latino voters, demographic determinism, and the myth of an inevitable democratic party majority. *Political Science Quarterly.* 139(3): 335–359. Oxford University Press (OUP). Epub ahead of print 15 March. https://doi.org/10.1093/PSQUAR/QQAE005 (May 19, 2024).

Database on Ideology, Money in Politics, and Elections (DIME): Public version 3.1 | Stanford Libraries Social Science Data Collection (n.d.). https://data.stanford.edu/dime (accessed March 12, 2024).

de la Garza RO and Cortina J (2007) Are Latinos Republicans but just don't know it?: The Latino vote in the 2000 and 2004 Presidential Elections. *American Politics Research* 35(2). SAGE: 202–223.

Despart Z and Svitek P (2022) For GOP, Winning Hispanic Voters Will Be a Bigger Fight than South Texas. www.texastribune.org/2022/10/21/texas-republican-democrat-hispanic-voters/ (accessed April 27, 2024).

Dovi S (2002) Preferable descriptive representatives: Will just any woman, black, or Latino do? *American Political Science Review* 96(4). Cambridge University Press: 729–743.

Dutwin D, Brodie M, Herrmann M, et al. (2005) Latinos and political party affiliation. *Hispanic Journal of Behavioral Sciences* 27(2): 135–160.

Fraga LR, Garcia JA, Hero RE, et al. (2010) *Latino Lives in America: Making It Home.* Philadelphia, PA: Temple University Press.

Fraga BL, Juenke EG, and Shah P (2020) Candidate Characteristics Cooperative (C3) 2018 Data. V2 ed. Harvard Dataverse. https://doi.org/10.7910/DVN/VHAPHV.

Fraga B, Velez YR, and West EA (2025) Reversion to the mean, or their version of the dream? Latino voting in an age of populism. *American Political Science Review* 119(1): 517–525. https://www.cambridge.org/core/journals/american-political-science-review/article/reversion-to-the-mean-or-their-version-of-the-dream-latino-voting-in-an-age-of-populism/D5FDF66C474541B3AABB4498BA59184C (accessed January 29, 2025).

Frederick B (2010) Gender and patterns of roll call voting in the U.S. Senate. *Congress & the Presidency* 37(2): 103–124. www.tandfonline.com/doi/abs/10.1080/07343460903390711 (accessed January 29, 2025).

Galbraith Q and Callister A (2020) Why would Hispanics vote for Trump? Explaining the controversy of the 2016 election. *Hispanic Journal of Behavioral Sciences* 42(1): 77–94.

Gallup (2024) Democrats Lose Ground with Black and Hispanic Adults. https://news.gallup.com/poll/609776/democrats-lose-ground-black-hispanic-adults.aspx (accessed May 14, 2024).

García JA (2005) *Latino Politics in America: Community, Culture, and Interests*. Rowman & Littlefield: 289.

Garcia J (2016) *Latino Politics in America: Community, Culture, and Interests*. Lanham, MD: Rowman and Littlefield.

Garcia FC and Sanchez GR (2015) Hispanics and the U.S. Political System: Moving into the Mainstream: 1–351. www.taylorfrancis.com/books/mono/10.4324/9781315664026/hispanics-political-system-chris-garcia-gabriel-sanchez (accessed January 29, 2025).

Gimpel JG and Kaufmann K (2001) Republican Efforts to Attract Latino Voters. https://cis.org/Report/Republican-Efforts-Attract-Latino-Voters (accessed May 19, 2024).

Girard C, Grenier GJ, and Gladwin H (2012) Exile politics and Republican Party affiliation: The case of Cuban Americans in Miami. *Social Science Quarterly (Wiley-Blackwell)* 93(1): 42–57.

Global Cleveland (2016) Bernie Moreno Interview. https://globalcleveland.org/bernie-moreno/ (accessed May 14, 2024).

González O (2024) Democrats Are Running Out of Time to Bring Back the Latino Voters They're Losing. www.notus.org/biden-2024/democrats-republicans-latino-voters (accessed May 14, 2024).

GOP basks in growing Latino outreach success | The Hill (n.d.). https://thehill.com/homenews/house/3558283-gop-sees-chance-to-steal-hispanic-voters-from-democrats/ (accessed April 16, 2024).

Greene W and Kim MS (2019) Hispanic Millennial Ideology: Surprisingly, No Liberal "Monolith" among College Students. *Hispanic Journal of Behavioral Sciences*. https://doi.org/10.1177/0739986319862829. 41(3). Los Angeles, CA: SAGE: 287–311.

Grossmann M and Hopkins DA (2024) Polarized by Degrees: How the Diploma Divide and the Culture War Transformed American Politics. Polarized by Degrees. https://www.cambridge.org/core/books/polarized-by-degrees/73B3136DC05749099EB07787A48FE522 (accessed January 29, 2025).

Grumbach JM (2022) *Laboratories against Democracy: How National Parties Transformed State Politics*. Princeton, NJ: Princeton University Press.

Gutiérrez RA (1987) The folklore of Spain in the American Southwest: Traditional Spanish Folk Literature in Northern New Mexico and Southern Colorado. *Hispanic American Historical Review* 67(1). Duke University Press: 149–150.

Hajnal ZL and Lee T (2011) What does it mean to be a partisan? In *Why Americans Don't Join the Party: Race, Immigration, and the Failure (of Political Parties) to Engage the Electorate*. Princeton: Princeton University Press: 145–178. https://press.princeton.edu/books/ebook/9781400838776/why-americans-dont-join-the-party-pdf (accessed January 29, 2025)

Hartig H (2023) 2022 US elections: Voting patterns by gender, race, education, age, party, religion | Pew Research Center. www.pewresearch.org/politics/2023/07/12/voting-patterns-in-the-2022-elections/ (accessed April 26, 2024).

Harvard-IOP (2024) Harvard Youth Poll – 47th Ed. – Spring. https://iop.harvard.edu/youth-poll/47th-edition-spring-2024 (accessed May 8, 2024).

Hero RE and Preuhs RR (2013) *Black–Latino Relations in U.S. National Politics: Beyond Conflict or Cooperation*. Cambridge: Cambridge University Press. www.cambridge.org/core/product/45BE86E2EB455FEEA369973E03183B8B.

Hero RE and Tolbert CJ (1995) Latinos and substantive representation in the U.S. House of Representatives: Direct, indirect, or nonexistent? *American Journal of Political Science* 39(3). Blackwell: 640–652.

Herrera J (2021) Why Democrats Are Losing Texas Latinos – Texas Monthly. www.texasmonthly.com/news-politics/democrats-losing-texas-latinos-trump/ (accessed April 27, 2024).

Herrera J (2022) Latinas Are Pushing a Political Revolution in South Texas – to the Right. www.texasmonthly.com/news-politics/republican-latinas-rio-grande-valley/ (accessed August 13, 2022).

Hill KA and Moreno D (1996) Second-Generation Cubans. *Hispanic Journal of Behavioral Sciences*. http://dx.doi.org/10.1177/07399863960182006 18(2). SAGE. 2455 Teller Road, Thousand Oaks, CA 91320: 175–193.

Huddy L, Mason L, and Horwitz SN (2016) Political identity convergence: On being Latino, becoming a democrat, and getting active. *Russell Sage Foundation* 2(3): 205–228.

Jardina A (2019) *White Identity Politics*. Cambridge: Cambridge University Press: 1–368.

Jiménez M (2013) *Inventive Politicians and Ethnic Ascent in American Politics: The Uphill Elections of Italians and Mexicans to the U.S. Congress*. New York City, NY: Taylor and Francis: 1–247.

Johnson JB and Secret PE (1996) Focus and style representational roles of congressional Black and Hispanic caucus members. *Journal of Black Studies* 26(3). SAGE: 245–273.

Jones-Correa M, Al-Faham H, and Cortez D (2018) Political (Mis)behavior: Attention and lacunae in the study of latino politics. *Annual Review of Sociology* 44: 213–235.

Judis JB and Teixeira RA (2002) *The Emerging Democratic Majority.* Scribner: 213.

Juenke EG (2014) Ignorance is bias: The effect of Latino losers on models of Latino representation. *American Journal of Political Science* 58(3). Midwest Political Science Association, Wiley: 593–603.

Kraushaar J (2022) Republicans Ramp up Focus on Hispanic Voters in Democratic Districts. www.axios.com/2022/07/24/republicans-hispanic-voters-districts (accessed August 28, 2022).

Krogstad J (2014) Census Bureau Lowers Forecasts for Hispanic Population Growth | Pew Research Center. www.pewresearch.org/short-reads/2014/12/16/with-fewer-new-arrivals-census-lowers-hispanic-population-projections-2/ (accessed May 19, 2024).

Lawless JL and Fox RL (2008) Why Are Women Still Not Running for Public Office? Epub ahead of print.

Lawless JL and Fox RL (2010) *It Still Takes a Candidate: Why Women Don't Run for office.* Cambridge: Cambridge University Press: 1–239.

Lawless JL and Fox RL (2018) *Women, Men & US Politics: Ten Big Questions.* NYC, NY: Norton: 214.

Lewis JB, Poole K, Rosenthal H, et al. (2022) Voteview: Congressional Roll-Call Votes Database.

Lonas L (2022) RNC Launches Program to Help Immigrants Prepare for Naturalization Test | The Hill. https://thehill.com/homenews/campaign/3559063-rnc-launches-program-to-help-immigrants-prepare-for-naturalization-test/ (accessed April 16, 2024).

Lublin D (1997) *The Paradox of Representation: Racial Gerrymandering and Minority Interests in Congress.* Princeton, NJ: Princeton University Press: 159.

Madrid M (2018) Puerto Rican Refugees and the Elusive Blue Wave. *The American Prospect* 29(2). Princeton, NJ: American Prospect PP – Princeton: 1–8.

Mansbridge J (1999) Should blacks represent blacks and women represent women? A contingent "yes." *Journal of Politics* 61(3). Chinese Corporation for Promotion of Humanities: 628–657.

Martinez M (2023a) Republicans Are Winning More Latino Votes. But Rising turnout Still Benefits Dems. – POLITICO. www.politico.com/news/2023/03/10/republicans-are-winning-more-latino-votes-but-rising-turnout-still-benefits-dems-00086361 (accessed April 26, 2024).

Martinez M (2023b) The "Relative Stability" of Conservative Latinos. www.politico.com/newsletters/the-recast/2023/09/29/latino-voter-population-conservatives-00119134 (accessed April 26, 2024).

Martinovich M (2017) Political Party Identities Stronger than Race or Religion. https://news.stanford.edu/2017/08/31/political-party-identities-stronger-race-religion/ (accessed May 8, 2024).

Mayhew DR (1974) *Congress: The Electoral Connection.* Yale University Press.

McManus J (2022) Latino voters are shifting to choosing Republican candidates. *The New American* 38(8): 9. https://link-gale-com.ezproxy.lib.uh.edu/apps/doc/A701930455/OVIC?u=txshracd2588&sid=bookmark-OVIC&xid=a1b01b63.

McNamee K (2022) Democrats Are Losing Latino Voters as Republicans Eye Opportunities at Midterms. www.npr.org/2022/10/24/1130451390/midterms-biden-democrats-republicans-latino-voters (accessed May 14, 2024).

Medina J (2024) Trump's Support among Latinos Grows, New Poll Shows. www.nytimes.com/2024/03/02/us/politics/trumps-support-among-latinos-grows-new-poll-shows.html (accessed April 26, 2024).

Messerly M and Diaz D (2024) Harris is changing the way Democrats target Latino voters. It's a risk. – POLITICO. www.politico.com/news/2024/09/22/harris-latino-voters-00180365 (accessed October 8, 2024).

Mirilovic N and Pollock III PH (2018) Latino Democrats, Latino Republicans and interest in country of origin politics. *Political Science Quarterly* 133(1). John Wiley & Sons: 127–149.

Moreno D (2006) Cuban political power: Challenge and consequences. *Cuban Affairs Quarterly* 2(1): (October, 2006). (Electronic Journal).

Morini M (2013) Congressional Hispanic Conference. In CE Cortes and JG Golson, (eds.), *Encyclopedia of Multicultural America.* New York: Sage: pp. 569–570. https://iris.uniroma1.it/handle/11573/1275542 (accessed May 19, 2024).

Mutnik A (2022) A key ingredient to flip the House: A wave of Latino GOP candidates – POLITICO. www.politico.com/news/2022/08/04/gop-latino-candidates-00049736 (accessed April 16, 2024).

Navarro-Rivera J (2022) Latinx Religion and Partisanship in the Post-Trump Era – Interfaith America. www.interfaithamerica.org/latinx-religion-and-partisanship-in-the-post-trump-era/ (accessed August 28, 2022).

Noe-Bustamante, Luis Martinez G, and Lopez MH (2022) Latinx Awareness Doubles among US Hispanics, but Few Use the Term | Pew Research Center. www.pewresearch.org/race-and-ethnicity/2024/09/12/latinx-awareness-has-doubled-among-u-s-hispanics-since-2019-but-only-4-percent-use-it/ (accessed October 8, 2024).

Pew Research Center (2018) Key Findings about Puerto Rico. www.pewresearch.org/fact-tank/2017/03/29/key-findings-about-puerto-rico/.

Pew Research Center (2021) American Trends Panel Wave 84. www.pewresearch .org/politics/dataset/american-trends-panel-wave-84/ (accessed August 28, 2022).

Phillips CD (2021) *Nowhere to Run: Race, Gender, and Immigration in American Elections*. Oxford: Oxford University Press: 1–264.

Philpot TS (2017) *Conservative but not Republican: The Paradox of Party Identification and Ideology among African Americans*: 1–281. https://www .cambridge.org/core/books/conservative-but-not-republican/87217C94E4F6 76B4A652EB00026EB7E9 (accessed January 29, 2025).

Pitkin HF (1967) *The Concept of Representation*. Oakland, CA: University of California Press: 1–324.

Reid T (2023) Hispanic Support for Trump Raises Red Flag for Biden. www .reuters.com/world/us/hispanic-support-trump-raises-red-flag-biden-2023- 12-16/ (accessed May 14, 2024).

Reingold B, Haynie KL, and Widner K (2020) *Race, Gender, and Political Representation: Toward a More Intersectional Approach*. Oxford: Oxford University Press: 1–232.

Riley J (2024) Why Democrats Are Losing Their Grip on Latino Voters. www .wsj.com/articles/why-democrats-are-losing-their-grip-on-hispanic-voters- 2024-election-fc42c582 (accessed May 14, 2024).

Root J (2012) George P. Bush Pushing GOP's Hispanic Outreach | The Texas Tribune. www.texastribune.org/2012/08/29/george-p-bush-pushing-his panic-outreach/ (accessed April 16, 2024).

Rouse SM (2013) *Latinos in the Legislative Process: Interests and Influence*. Cambridge: Cambridge University Press. https://books.google.com/books/ about/Latinos_in_the_Legislative_Process.html?id=AdK6Z1RYa4gC (accessed May 19, 2024).

RSLC (2022a) GOP Steps up Hispanic State Legislator Push. www.rslc.gop/in- the-news/x3kzjcveom2sfg9eyna5nib5h9sp3t (accessed October 8, 2024).

RSLC (2022b) The Hill: GOP Extends Hispanic Outreach to Down-Ballot State Races. www.rslc.gop/in-the-news/the-hill-gop-extends-hispanic-outreach- to-down-ballot-state-races (accessed April 16, 2024).

Saavedra Cisneros A (2016) *Latino Identity and Political Attitudes: Why Are Latinos Not Republican*. New York: Palgrave MacMillan Press.

Salomon G and Torrens C (2018) US Mainland Politicians Wooing Puerto Ricans: WHO FLED STORM. *The Hispanic Outlook in Higher Education* 28(9). Paramus: The Hispanic Outlook in Higher Education PP – Paramus: 30–31.

Sanchez B (2022) The Latino Voter Shift Comes into Focus in South Texas. CNN. www.cnn.com/2022/10/14/politics/latino-voters-texas-15th/index .html (accessed April 27, 2024).

Sanchez GR and Masuoka N (2010) Brown-Utility Heuristic? The Presence and Contributing Factors of Latino Linked Fate. *Hispanic Journal of Behavioral Sciences.* http://dx.doi.org/10.1177/0739986310383129. 32(4). Los Angeles, CA: SAGE: 519–531.

Shah PR, Juenke EG, and Fraga BL (2022) Here comes everybody: Using a data cooperative to understand the new dynamics of representation. *PS: Political Science & Politics* 55(2). March 31. Cambridge University Press: 300–302.

Shor B and McCarty N (2011) The ideological mapping of American Legislatures. *The American Political Science Review* 105(3). American Political Science Association, Cambridge University Press: 530–551.

Shor B and McCarty N (2023) Individual State Legislator Shor-McCarty Ideology Data, April Update. V1 ed. Harvard Dataverse. https://doi.org/ 10.7910/DVN/NWSYOS.

Stewart C (2022) The Democratic Party Is Shedding Latino Voters. Here's Why. *The New Republic.* https://newrepublic.com/article/166406/democrats-los ing-latino-voters-2022?utm_medium=Social&utm_campaign=EB_TNR& utm_source=Twitter#Echobox=1652281606-3 (accessed August 13, 2022).

Stokes-Brown AK (2012) America's shifting color line? Reexamining determinants of Latino racial self-identification*. *Social Science Quarterly* 93(2). John Wiley & Sons: 309–332.

Stokes-Brown AK (2018) The Latino vote in the 2016 election – myths and realities about the "Trump Effect." In J Lucas, C Galdieri, and T Sisco (eds.), *Conventional Wisdom, Parties, and Broken Barriers in the 2016 Election.* Lanham, MD: Lexington Books: 61–80.

Stout CT and Garcia JR (2014) The big tent effect: Descriptive candidates and black and Latino political partisanship. *American Politics Research* 43(2). SAGE: 205–231.

Svitek P (2021) Democratic Texas Rep. Ryan Guillen Switches to GOP after Redistricting | The Texas Tribune. www.texastribune.org/2021/11/15/ryan-guillen-texas-house-switch-party/ (accessed May 18, 2024).

Svitek P (2022) John Lujan and Frank Ramirez vie for San Antonio-area Texas House Seat. www.texastribune.org/2022/11/04/texas-house-district-118-2022-election/ (accessed May 14, 2024).

Swain CM (1993) *Black Faces, Black Interests: The Representation of African Americans in Congress.* Cambridge, MA: Harvard University Press: 275.

Swers ML (2013) *Women in the Club: Gender and Policy Making in the Senate.* https://press.uchicago.edu/ucp/books/book/chicago/W/bo15233103.html. Chicago University Press. Chicago, IL.

Tate K (2001) The political representation of blacks in Congress: Does race matter? *Legislative Studies Quarterly* 26: 623–638.

Teixeira R (2023) Why Hispanic Voters Are a Growing Challenge for Democrats in 2024. www.washingtonpost.com/opinions/2023/07/05/hispanic-voters-gop-biden/ (accessed April 26, 2024).

Thomsen DM (2015) Ideological Moderates Won't Run: How Party Fit Matters for Partisan Polarization in Congress. *The Journal of Politics* 76(3): 786–797.

UnidosUS (2023) Survey of Latino Voters in Texas. Epub ahead of print.

Vigil JD (1938-) *From Indians to Chicanos: The Dynamics of Mexican American Culture*: Long Grove, Ill., Waveland Press, 2012.

Vigil ME (1996) *Hispanics in Congress: A Historical and Political Survey.* Millburn, NJ: University Press of America: 127.

Ward M (2024) Biden Steps up Hispanic Outreach as Warning Signs Flash – POLITICO. www.politico.com/news/2024/04/21/biden-trump-hispanic-vote-2024-00153518 (accessed May 19, 2024).

Westwood SJ, Iyengar S, Walgrave S, et al. (2018) The tie that divides: Cross-national evidence of the primacy of partyism. *European Journal of Political Research* 57(2). John Wiley & Sons: 333–354.

White A, Juenke EG, and Fraga BL (2022) Evaluating the Minority Candidate Penalty with a Regression Discontinuity Approach. Epub ahead of print.

Wilson WC (2017) *From Inclusion to Influence: Latino Representation in Congress and Latino Political Incorporation in America.* Ann Arbor, MI: University of Michigan Press. Epub ahead of print September 29. https://doi.org/10.3998/MPUB.8918784.

Wineinger CN (2022) *Gendering the GOP: Intraparty Politics and Republican Women's Representation in Congress*: 1–220. https://academic.oup.com/book/38819 (January 29, 2025).

Winter M (2021) Latinos Will Determine the Future of American Evangelicalism. www.theatlantic.com/culture/archive/2021/07/latinos-will-determine-future-american-evangelicalism/619551/.

Wroe Andrew (2008) *The Republican Party and Immigration Politics: From Proposition 187 to George W. Bush.* New York: Palgrave Macmillan.

Zhou L (2022) A Record Number of Latina Republicans Are Running for Congress in 2022 – Vox. www.vox.com/the-highlight/23329428/latina-republican-candidates-2022-red-wave (accessed April 16, 2024).

Zitner A (2021) Hispanic Voters in This Pennsylvania City Are Shifting Toward the GOP. Both Parties Want to Know Why. www.wsj.com/articles/hispanic-voters-in-this-pennsylvania-city-are-shifting-toward-the-gop-both-parties-want-to-know-why-11640687403 (accessed April 26, 2024).

Acknowledgements

We decided to write this Element to provide an objective and data-driven analysis of what we were observing in American politics in recent years. As more Latino Republicans were running and winning office, we wanted to know why, and we were fortunate to be involved with the Candidate Characteristics Cooperative (C3) team led by Bernard Fraga, Paru Shah, and Eric Gonzalez Juenke. This exciting new dataset gave us the opportunity to answer important research questions in the study of Latino representation. For both of us, writing this Element has been transformative, and it would not have been possible without the support, encouragement, and inspiration from many incredible individuals.

First, we extend our deepest gratitude to our families and friends, who helped us often with their own opinions about what they thought about our findings, often very different from what our political science colleagues observed.

A heartfelt thank you to Frances Lee, whose confidence in our project was apparent from the start and whose attention to detail and thoughtful suggestions helped shape this Element into its final form. Your expertise and dedication have been instrumental in bringing this project to life.

We would also like to acknowledge our colleagues at the University of Houston, whose encouragement have significantly influenced our writing journey. We are grateful for the many informal conversations and presentations about our work. In addition, Casellas thanks the Rothermere American Institute and Balliol College who provided a home away from home during his sabbatical where he was able to work on this Element and bounce ideas off of people from all disciplines.

We are immensely grateful to the anonymous reviewers, discussants, and colleagues who gave us feedback on our early drafts and helped us focus our findings. In particular, we thank Alexandra Filindra, Tony Affigne, Kostanca Dhima, Andra Gillespie, Jamil Scott, Fernando Tormos-Aponte, Loren Collingwood, Rula Jabbour, participants at the Winant Lecture at Oxford's Rothermere American Institute, Balliol College's lecture series, and the Nuffield College seminar.

Lastly, we hope this Element will spark conversations, inspire new research, and lead to a greater understanding of one of the most interesting developments in American politics in the past several years. Thank you.

Cambridge Elements ≡

American Politics

Elements in the Series

American Affective Polarization in Comparative Perspective
Noam Gidron, James Adams and Will Horne

The Study of US State Policy Diffusion: What Hath Walker Wrought?
Christopher Z. Mooney

Why Bad Policies Spread (and Good Ones Don't)
Charles R. Shipan and Craig Volden

*The Partisan Next Door: Stereotypes of Party Supporters and Consequences
for Polarization in America*
Ethan C. Busby, Adam J. Howat, Jacob E. Rothschild and Richard M. Shafranek

The Dynamics of Public Opinion
Mary Layton Atkinson, K. Elizabeth Coggins, James A. Stimson and Frank
R. Baumgartner

The Origins and Consequences of Congressional Party Election Agendas
Scott R. Meinke

*The Full Armor of God: The Mobilization of Christian Nationalism in American
Politics*
Paul A. Djupe, Andrew R. Lewis and Anand E. Sokhey

*The Dimensions and Implications of the Public's Reactions to the January 6, 2021,
Invasion of the U.S. Capitol*
Gary C. Jacobson

*Cooperating Factions: A Network Analysis of Party Divisions
in U.S Presidential Nominations*
Rachel M. Blum and Hans C. Noel

*The Haves and Have-Nots in Supreme Court Representation and Participation,
2016 to 2021*
Kirsten Widner and Anna Gunderson

The Political Dynamics of Partisan Polarization
Eric R. Schmidt, Edward G. Carmines and Paul M. Sniderman

*Shifting Allegiances: The Election of Latino Republicans to Congress and State
Legislatures*
Robert D. Alvarez and Jason P. Casellas

A full series listing is available at: www.cambridge.org/EAMP

www.ingramcontent.com/pod-product-compliance
Ingram Content Group UK Ltd.
Pitfield, Milton Keynes, MK11 3LW, UK
UKHW020846180525
458533UK00011B/98